The
Native People
of
Alaska

W9-BRX-325

Steve J. Langdon

**Historic photos from various collections
Anchorage Museum of History and Art**

Greatland Graphics   **Anchorage**

Acknowledgement   I have been aided in a number of ways in the preparation of this book. First I would like to thank all the Native people who have educated me and welcomed me into their homes in various parts of Alaska during the past decade and a half. It is my hope that this book will contribute to a wider appreciation of their traditional culture and present aspirations. Second I would like to thank Diane Brenner of the Anchorage Museum of History and Art for her assistance in identifying the photos which appear in the book. Finally thanks to Ed Bovy for his enthusiasm and editorial assistance.

A portion of the author's proceeds from this book will be directed to Alaska Native organizations working to maintain traditional values, self-determination and ancestral lands for future generations of Alaska Natives.

S.L.
April, 1987

Publisher	Greatland Graphics ©1987
Printing	Lorraine Press
Typography	Visible Ink
Edit/design	Edward Bovy
Cartography/art	Kathy Kiefer

Front cover	Inupiat man and his grandson (Photo by Kathy Kiefer)
Facing page	Eskimo berry pickers, circa 1910, Nome

Contents

1. Introduction. 4

2. Aleuts 10

3. Northern Eskimos: Inupiat 22

4. Southern Eskimos: Yuit. 34

5. Interior Indians 48

6. Southeast Coastal Indians: Tlingit and Haida. 60

7. Historic Change. 72

References. 80

CHAPTER 1

Introduction

Alaska, the great northwestern subcontinent of North America, is home to a unique and diverse group of aboriginal people. This book is an introduction to their culture and history.

Alaska's indigenous people, who are jointly called Alaska Natives, can be divided into five major groupings: Aleuts, Northern Eskimos (Inupiat), Southern Eskimos (Yuit), Interior Indians (Athabascans) and Southeast Coastal Indians (Tlingit and Haida). These groupings are based on broad cultural and linguistic similarities of peoples living contiguously in different regions of Alaska. They do not represent political or tribal units nor are they the units Native people have traditionally used to define themselves. At the time of contact with Russian explorers in the mid-18th century, Alaska was occupied by approximately 80,000 indigenous people. The phrase "time of contact" means the earliest time when a Native group had significant direct interaction with Europeans. This time varied for different parts of Alaska; therefore Alaskan Native groups have had somewhat different historical experiences through their contact with Europeans and Americans.

Time of Contact for Alaskan Native Groups

Aleut	1750-1780
Southern Eskimo	1780-1840
Northern Eskimo	1850-1870
Interior Indians	1840-1860
Coastal Indians	1775-1800

Alaskan Environments

Alaska is a huge landmass which encompasses a number of diverse environments. It is a land of harsh extremes from 250 inches of rainfall annually, to –80° F in the dead of winter, to howling gales with winds in excess of 100 knots. For those living above the Arctic Circle (60°N), there are days in the summer when the sun doesn't go down and nights in the winter when the sun doesn't rise. The 533,000 square miles of Alaska

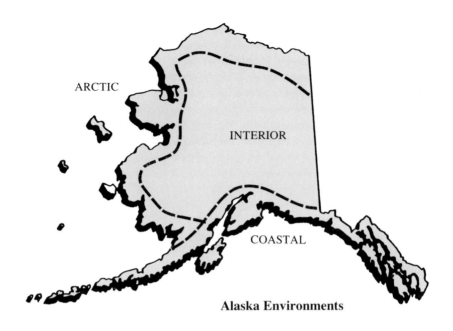

Alaska Environments

are spread over nearly 20 degrees of latitude. Alaska is bounded on three sides by water and its total coastline of 33,000 miles is as long as that of the rest of the United States.

But Alaska is blessed with abundant fish and wildlife which with knowledge and care can provide for many people. Many migratory species travel to Alaska in the summer to give birth to their offspring making this season extremely vital for food production. Marine resources are especially abundant in the Bering Sea while Alaska's two major rivers, the Yukon and Kuskokwim, drain thousands of square miles of interior Alaska, providing habitat for many fish species.

There are three major environments in Alaska where climatic conditions, flora and fauna are similar. In the south, along the North Pacific coast, the climate is mild and damp due to the influence of the warm Japanese Current from the tropics. There is relatively little seasonal variation in this region with winter temperatures rarely falling below freezing and summer temperatures rarely rising above 60° F. From Kodiak Island eastward in this region is the temperate rain forest where stands of Sitka spruce, cedar and hemlock form towering and impenetrable forests. West of Kodiak Island to the tip of the Aleutians, long grasses and shrubs are the major flora.

5

Extending in a two-hundred mile wide band around the western and northern coast of Alaska from Bristol Bay to the Canadian border is the Arctic region. Cold winters and cool summers are characteristic with northern regions experiencing more intensity in winter cold than southern. *Tundra*, composed of ground-hugging flora such as mosses, lichens, sedges and shrubs with few or no trees, is found throughout the Arctic.

The third Alaskan environment is the interior which lies south of the Brooks Range, north of the Alaska Range and east of the coastal strip of Arctic environment. It is dominated by the Yukon River whose many tributaries drain the interior. Cold winters, with temperatures frequently below $-50°$ F are offset by short, hot summers with temperatures occasionally above $90°$ F, thunderstorms and forest fires. The *boreal forest*, consisting of relatively small specimens of white and black spruce, alder, birch and aspen, covers most of the rolling hills characteristic of interior terrain. Immense marshy, flatlands, prime habitat for waterfowl, are found in bottomlands of many of the rivers.

This "Great Land" is the deeply revered home for Native people who have accepted it on its own terms and successfully adapted their lifestyles to it for more than 500 generations.

Prehistory   Alaska has a special place in human history as the likely route by which the New World came to be occupied. Most archeologists believe that migration into the New World occurred sometime (perhaps more than once) between 50,000 and 15,000 years ago during the last ice age. During that time sea level was as much as 350 feet lower than now. This linked Siberia and western Alaska into a huge arctic grassland called *Beringia*. An early wave of migrants, called *Paleo-Indians*, probably came into this region in pursuit of mammoth, mastodon and other large herbivores. They are generally believed to have passed through Alaska, travelling southward to occupy North, Central and South America within several thousand years after first entering the New World. The ancestors of contemporary Alaska Natives are thought to be part of later movements of people into the New World from 5–10,000 years ago. One hypothesis is that two episodes of immigration occurred, an earlier wave of Indians about 7–9,000 years ago and a later wave of Eskimos 6–7,000 years ago. However, there is little agreement about when the earliest migration occurred, how many other migrations occurred or where in Beringia they occurred.

The oldest archeological materials which conclusively demonstrate human occupation of Alaska come from Trail Creeks Cave north of Nome where a cracked bison leg bone and a bone point, later dated as 15,000 years old, were found. Evidence for human occupation after 11,000 years ago is much better. Small stone hunting tools, known as microblades have been found in virtually all parts of Alaska except Prince William Sound and Kodiak Island. No evidence of housing structures has been found with these tools; it is believed that the makers were nomadic hunters and gatherers who pursued a variety of mammals including caribou and bison. The distribution of these artifacts indicates people gradually spread throughout Alaska between 11,000 and 7,000 years ago.

Early Alaskans altered their adaptations after 7,000 years ago. Two tendencies are apparent: regional styles of tools and artifacts emerge and the microblade type tools give way to larger projectile points. It is has been suggested that this shift parallels a change in the environment in which the boreal forest replaced grasslands in much of Alaska.

About 4,000 years ago, the *Arctic Small Tool Tradition* appeared in western Alaska and spread eastward across the arctic region of Canada to Greenland. Because of its distribution, this tool tradition is considered characteristic of the earliest Eskimo population. The maritime focus on seals, walrus, and whales emerged and subsequent stages of Eskimo culture developed and refined it to great sophistication.

After 4,000 years ago, the archeological record becomes much more complicated as innovations in housing types, tool types, artistic styles and burial styles occurred all over Alaska. The number and size of sites increase indicating an expanding population. Regional variations become relatively distinct and apparently lead to the artifacts and cultural patterns characteristic of Alaska Native groups at contact. It must be emphasized, however, that the archeology of Alaska remains poorly understood and much work remains to be done to reveal the story of Alaskan prehistory.

Languages   Alaska Native languages fall into two major *language families*, that is groups of languages which are related. These are *Eska-Aleutian* and *Na-Dene*. Languages in the Eska-Aleutian family are separated into Aleut and Eskimo. Eskimo is further subdivided into Inupiaq and Yup'ik. The difference between these two languages is roughly the same as between English and German. The boundary between the two languages groups occurs just north of the mouth of the Yukon

7

River. From there north on the North American mainland and on Little Diomede Island, Inupiaq is spoken all the way to Greenland in a series of mutually understandable dialects. Yup'ik is subdivided further into three major mutually incomprehensible languages:

- Siberian Yup'ik spoken by the St. Lawrence Island and Siberian Eskimos;
- Central Yup'ik spoken by a number of groups on the Alaskan mainland from the mouth of the Yukon River south and east to the Alaska Peninsula;
- Alutiiq spoken along the southside of the Alaska Peninsula, on Kodiak Island, on the lower part of the Kenai Peninsula and in Prince William Sound.

Languages change when speakers of the same language are isolated from each other. It is estimated that Aleut and the proto-Eskimo language separated 6–7,000 years ago. Yup'ik and Inupiaq have been separated for about 2,000 years with less time separating the Yup'ik languages.

The Na-Dene language family includes the Athabascan languages, Eyak and probably Tlingit. Also included in the Na-Dene family are a number of Athabascan languages in northern Canada, British Columbia, and California as well as Apache and Navajo of the southwestern United States. In Alaska, 12 separate Athabascan languages are recognized. Linguistic evidence suggests Tlingit may have diverged from the other languages as long as 6,000 years ago. For the remainder of the Alaskan Athabascan languages, constant contact among speakers produces a unique situation where distinct languages are recognized yet mutual comprehensibility between speakers is relatively high. Eyak and Tlingit speakers, on the other hand, cannot be understood by speakers of Athabascan languages.

Physical Characteristics

Alaskan Eskimos are closely related genetically to Siberian peoples such as the Chukchi. In general they are heavy-boned, muscular and lean. They have relatively small hands and relatively short legs in proportion to their height. They are short to medium in stature with Inupiat populations tending to be considerably taller than Yup'ik populations. Their skin color is quite light and weathers to an olive shade with exposure. They have large heads with relatively flat faces, low-bridged noses, high cheekbones and epicanthic folds in their eyelids. Hair is straight and dark brown to black with little body hair and minimal facial hair among men.

Recent studies indicate that Eskimos have several possible genetic adaptations to cold. Brown adipose fat tissue

Eskimos in ceremonial costume, Cape Prince of Wales. Drums were made from seal intestine stretched across a wooden frame.

is retained into adulthood in Eskimo populations whereas it is only found in childhood in other human populations. This tissue is metabolized to sustain core body temperatures under cold stress. Hands and feet of Eskimos appear to show greater and more rapid vasoconstriction and dilation than other human populations allowing for greater blood flow thus maintaining higher temperatures in the hands and feet. Contrary to popular belief, Eskimos do not have more fat than other people.

Alaskan Indians tend to be more closely related genetically to other American Indians than they are to Alaskan Eskimos. Alaskan Indian populations tend to be medium to tall in stature with long arms, short trunks and long legs. In general, they are angular and moderately built. Skin color is relatively light, darkening to olive or brown under exposure. All have relatively large heads with broad faces but not as broad as Eskimos. Epicanthic folds are occasionally apparent. Hair is straight and coarse from dark brown to black in color; body hair is minimal with moderate amounts of facial hair among males.

Tlingit and Haida tend to be stockier with broad muscular chests and shoulders compared to Athabascans. Athabascans tend to have noses with higher bridges while Tlingit and Haida noses tend to be flatter.

9

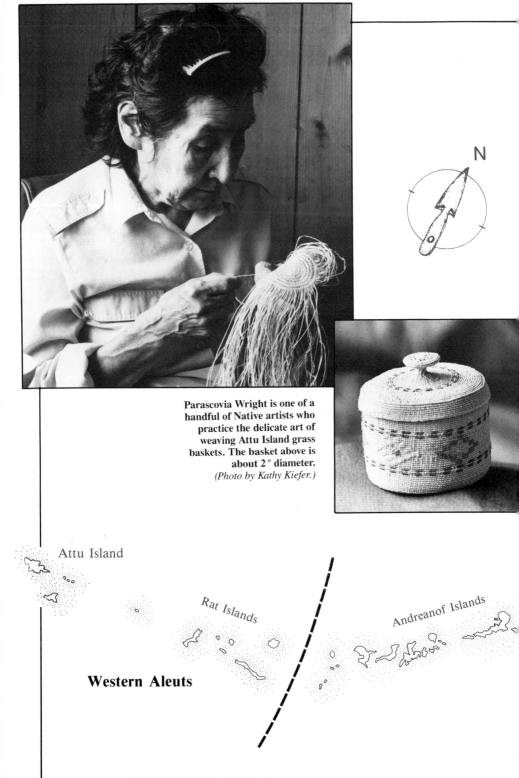

N

Parascovia Wright is one of a
handful of Native artists who
practice the delicate art of
weaving Attu Island grass
baskets. The basket above is
about 2″ diameter.
(Photo by Kathy Kiefer.)

Attu Island

Rat Islands

Andreanof Islands

Western Aleuts

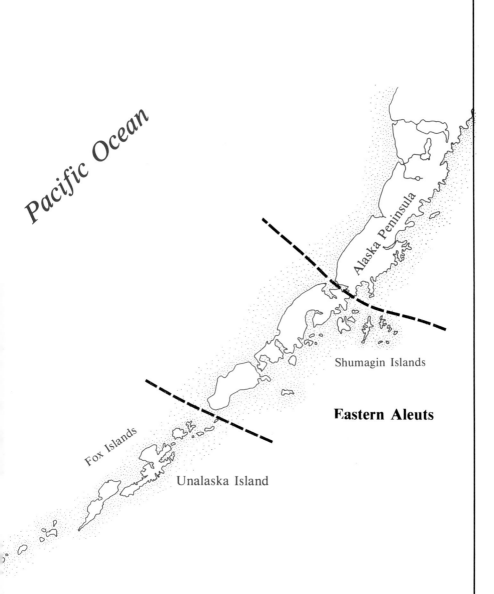

Pacific Ocean

Alaska Peninsula

Shumagin Islands

Eastern Aleuts

Fox Islands

Unalaska Island

Central Aleuts

Aleuts

CHAPTER 2

Aleuts

Stretching like a rocky necklace from Asia to North America, the Aleutian Islands and the nearby Alaska Peninsula are the home of the Aleut. The term "Aleut" was introduced by Russians and comes originally from the Koryak or Chukchi languages of Siberia; it appears to have been quickly adopted by the Aleut people themselves (Lantis 1985).

The Aleut are distinctive among the world's people for their remarkably successful maritime adaptation to this cold archipelago. Some archeologists suggest that contemporary Aleuts are the descendants of a population which first established itself at Anangula Island more than 7,000 years ago. At the time of European contact, the Aleut population inhabited all of the major Aleutian Islands, the Alaska Peninsula as far east as Port Moller, and the Shumagin Islands to the south of the Alaska Peninsula.

Although reconstruction of Aleut culture and history is difficult due to the devastating impact of Russian contact in the 18th century, it is believed that the Aleuts were divided into nine named subdivisions. The total Aleut population is estimated to have been between 15–18,000 people at the time of contact. The nine subdivisions are usually joined into western, central and eastern groups based on language. Population concentration was greatest among the eastern groups who had access to salmon and caribou. The Aleuts were a relatively long-lived people with a considerable proportion of the population more than 60 years of age.

Settlements   Aleut settlements included villages and seasonal camps. Winter villages, which could be used year round, were generally placed in protected locations along the shoreline with a good beach, a nearby freshwater stream, a headland for observation and close proximity to marine mammals, fish and intertidal resources. On the mainland, settlements tended to be on the southside of the Alaska Peninsula, perhaps to avoid winter ice from the Bering Sea, while in the Aleutian Islands, settlements often were located on the north side, probably to avoid the prevailing southwest winds. A typical village consisted of about 200 people living in five to ten dwellings. Tents or abandoned houses were used at seasonal camps where people gathered food.

Houses

The basic house of the Aleut is called a *barabara* (a Siberian term). Barabaras were oblong pit dwellings with wooden or whale bone frames and rafters overlain by grass and sod. Often they were nearly indistinguishable from the surrounding terrain. Barabaras were normally entered by means of a pole ladder through an entryway in the ceiling. Their typical dimensions were 35 to 40 feet long by 20 to 30 feet wide with the floor being four to six feet below ground level. The inside consisted of an open space in the middle portion for general living and compartments with trenches along the walls for sleeping. These were separated by grass mats hung from the rafters. Sometimes compartments were dug into the earthwalls for burials.

Tools, baskets and other objects were manufactured in the open area. A trough of urine was kept there. Uric acid was used by most Alaskan Native groups for purposes like washing hair (a freshwater rinse would be used afterward), softening skins or making dyes.

Aleut houses were heated by oil lamps and occasionally small hearths. Most cooking was done outside the home near storage and refuse pits. Apparently there were no large community houses or steambaths in Aleut villages.

Unga Island, Alaska, 1914. The treeless windswept Aleutian Islands were first colonized by the Aleuts more than 7000 years ago. The steep rocky shores made the occasional flat sandy beach a valuable site for settlement.

Food and diet   The most important animal to the Aleut was the Steller sea lion. This animal provided not only food but also a vast variety of other products including boat covers (hide), line and cord (sinew), oil (blubber), tools (bones), fishhooks (teeth), boot soles (flippers), containers (stomach) and materials for garments (esophagus and intestines). Other important marine mammals were seals, sea otter and whales which together with the sea lion comprised 50 percent of the diet.

Aleut whaling was a highly ritualized activity for which men and their wives prepared themselves by abstinence and other behaviors to make themselves worthy. Men hunted whales alone from kayaks with harpoons. The stone harpoon heads were coated with a "magical" poison concocted from the aconite plant. Once wounded, the whale could live several days to a week as the "poison" slowly worked. During this time the hunter who struck the whale secluded himself in his house and pretended to be ill hoping that the whale likewise would become sick and die. Other hunters would watch the whale to see what happened. If the whale died nearby, it was towed to the beach. Whales wounded but lost were often recovered by other Aleuts when they washed ashore.

Not all Aleuts engaged in whaling. In the central and eastern areas, Aleuts hunted caribou and fished for salmon. Aleut fishermen caught halibut and cod with ingenious wooden hooks and line made of braided kelp or sea lion sinew.

Women, children and the elderly concentrated on collecting bird eggs, intertidal organisms (such as chitons, clams, sea urchins and seaweed) and plants, roots and berries which ripened in the late summer and fall.

Societal roles   Aleuts are world famous for their unparalleled skill in handling the *baidarka* (or kayak), the distinctive skin boat they mastered. Males trained from an early age in the skills necessary to hunt, handle watercraft and survive in rough waters surrounding the Aleutian Islands. One of their most impressive skills was the righting of a capsized baidarka while still in it. Aleuts also used the *baidar*, a large open skin boat, for travel and trade.

The training of an Aleut male from his youth included the systematic stretching of leg and shoulder muscles. This enabled him to endure the long hours of concentration and stillness necessary if the arduous and time-consuming pursuit of seals and sea otter was to be successful. The boy's shoulder muscles had to be strengthened to achieve maximum velocity and accuracy with the throwing board or *atlatl* which was used to cast darts and harpoons at birds and marine mammals.

The traditional Aleut house, the barabara, was a sod-covered dugout typically entered through a hole in the roof. This barabara's door indicates Russian influence. *(From the Healy Collection, Henry E. Huntington Library.)*

Despite the cultural emphasis on male hardiness and self-reliance, there was a recognized role in Aleut society for the male transvestite (or *berdache*) who dressed and worked as a woman.

Aleut women were trained from early childhood in the important sewing, weaving and food processing skills. In later life this training would insure that their husbands were appropriately outfitted for hunting. Aleut basketry made from the fine grasses of the islands as well as from spruce roots is some of the best in the world.

Clothing and decoration

Aleut women constructed marvelous waterproof *kamleikas* (men's outer garments) by painstakingly stitching together strips of sea lion intestine. Waterproof boots were made from sea otter flippers. Colorful cloaks for ceremonial occasions were crafted from the skins of hundreds of tufted puffins taken with snares. Women commonly wore luxurious capes and garments of sea otter fur.

Distinctive elements of Aleut clothing were the beautiful visors and elongate hats worn by the men. Functional designs worn for daily use kept the incessant rain off the hunter and protected his eyes from the ocean's glare. Elegant ceremonial hats were painted in striped curving designs of different colors, often with sea lion whiskers attached for additional decoration.

Supplementary personal adornment existed for both men and women. Simple tatoos, usually short straight lines, were inscribed on the hands and faces. Nose pins were worn

"Habitans des îles Aléoutiennes."

"Inhabitants of the Aleutian Islands," hand colored lithograph circa 1825 by Louis Choris (1795-1828). The distinctive Aleut visors were made from wood and had sea lion whiskers for decoration. The visors shielded a hunter's face from sun and rain.

Aleut dancing masks have been found in burials in the Shumagin and Aleutian islands. Note the holes on the edges to attach the mask to the head.

by men and women. Labrets, flat circular discs made of wood or ivory, were inserted into slits in the area between the lower lip and the chin. A common style was to wear one below each corner of the mouth. The labret is an extremely old adornment, appearing more than 4,000 years ago in the Aleut cultural record. It is no longer worn.

Kinship patterns

Matrilineal (traced through the female) descent and inheritance determined Aleut kinship patterns. Although a house was owned by a woman, usually her brothers and their wives were the primary occupants. A recognized leader of the house, usually the eldest male, made most decisions for the group. Children, particularly males, lived with their mothers during infancy but moved in mid-childhood to the home of their mother's brother. This practice, termed the *avunculate*, makes the uncle the primary teacher and trainer of his sister's children. The uncle's role was generally a strict one in order to insure the competence of the young man. The boy's father assumed a sympathetic, reassuring and supportive role.

Most marriages were monogamous although *polygyny* (multiple wives) occurred among wealthier, more powerful leaders. Divorce was possible although rare in Aleut society; when desired, a woman simply returned to her own home or that of her eldest sister.

There is little evidence of more complex social organization among the Aleut beyond the house-group. There were no men's houses and probably no clans. Although each house group was apparently independent, a senior or leading house in a community was recognized and its leader was considered the village leader. The Russians introduced the term *toyon* for this person. Coordination of movement to camps by several house groups and even the village occurred periodically since villages were composed of closely related people. The village leader was primarily responsible for decisions concerning war and peace.

Social organization

Aleut society was roughly divided into three classes — wealthy people, common people and slaves (Lantis 1985). The wealthy and common people were usually closely related, thus minimizing conflict. Only whale hunting and possibly leadership were inherited. The number of slaves, primarily women, is thought to have been small.

Although there was no formal village organization, Aleut communities claimed certain areas as their resource territories such as rookeries, fishing banks and beaches.

These areas would be closely watched. Other Aleuts using those areas were considered trespassers if they had not requested access. Normally, however, people would simply go to the nearest village where customs of generosity would ensure that they would be well fed. Poachers could be evicted or attacked.

Warfare was not uncommon among the Aleut. Accounts tell of battles waged over long distance with the Koniag people of Kodiak Island, the Eskimo groups of the Alaska Peninsula and even the Chugach in Prince William Sound. Slat armor constructed of tightly woven wooden rods have been found; however, Aleut legends state that only the head of a household wore armor (Laughlin 1980). Hostilities often took the form of raids in which small groups of men, usually less than 10, attacked another village to avenge some insult or theft or to obtain women as slaves.

Russian Orthodox church, Nushegak, Alaska, 1900. The influence of the Russian Church alleviated many abuses against the Aleuts. Russian Orthodoxy is still a major religion among the Aleut, Koniag, and Chugach today.

Ceremonies   Good relationships were maintained between communities through winter festivities of dancing and feasting. The village chief from one village would invite another village to visit.

18

The visitors would arrive in their best clothing and were housed and fed generously by their hosts. After changing into ceremonial costumes, dancers with tambourine drums from each group took turns trying to outperform each other. Women danced while shaking rattles made of inflated bladders. Wooden masks were used in some dances to invoke the presence of powerful spirits. Distinctive wooden masks with exceptionally large, broad noses and a slightly wolf-like appearance have been found in burials in different parts of Aleut territory. Wrestling and storytelling were also favorite entertainments with exceptional performers given respect and honored status.

Occasions of special significance and ceremony in the Aleut life cycle were marriage, puberty and especially death. Following most deaths, viscera were removed and the body cavity stuffed with grass. Then the person would be propped up in the corner of the house on a mat specially woven for them or placed in wooden cradle-like frame suspended over the normal sleeping place. There the corpse would remain for as long as several months. People felt no horror of the dead but rather a deep sense of loss and wished to prolong the presence of the deceased. Most of the dead were then buried in the house walls or under the floor. Another form of burial, mummification, was unique among the Aleut. It was apparently practiced only in the eastern and central areas and associated with whaling specialists.

Beliefs Although little is known of the Aleut belief system, they appear to have conceived of a creator deity related to the sun who was instrumental in hunting success and the reincarnation of souls. Small images of the creator, known as *kaathaagaathagh*, were carved from ivory and hung from the ceiling beams (Laughlin 1980). The creator, however, had little impact on everyday life which was instead influenced by two classes of spirits, good and evil. Animals also had spirits. The most important ones were those of the whale and sea otter. Aleut men wore a variety of amulets and charms that were thought to provide special powers from the animal spirits to enhance success in hunting. The Aleuts believed in the reincarnation of souls which migrated between the earth, a world below and a world above.

Behavior patterns Aleut life was laid out in a clear and dignified manner. Appropriate behaviors were taught and reinforced from early childhood. Aleuts did not speak unless something important needed to be said. Men kept silent lookout vigils for hours

19

Aleut Mummies

The special importance of death and the spirit of the deceased is apparent in the distinctive mummification practices of the Aleuts. On Kagamil Island, an amazing 234 excellently preserved bodies have been discovered in several caves. According to William Laughlin, a widely recognized expert on the Aleuts, mummification was practiced to preserve the spiritual power which resides in each person. These powers could be solicited at a later time by emboldened Aleut hunters who visited the caves and took a bit of flesh from one of the mummies, hoping it would bring assistance in whaling. But this was dangerous and those who sought such power might be subject to insanity, severe sickness and early death. Even the kin of whalers who sought the power of the mummies could suffer harm from the spirit forces unleashed.

Scientific studies have revealed a detailed Aleut understanding of human anatomy. Mummification is dependent on two factors: deactivating tissue destroying enzymes in the body and halting invasion of the body by microorganisms that decompose the flesh and soft tissue. Both are best accomplished by warmth and dryness as found in the arid regions of Egypt and Chile. The Aleuts controlled these processes by extracting the viscera from the body, inserting dry grass into the cavity and constantly drying the body for up to a month after death. The body was kept in a flexed position bent at the knees. Prior to entombment, the body was wrapped first with multiple layers of seal or sea lion intestine, then with clothing and finally with skins or mats. Often it was placed in a wooden cradle or upon a raised platform in the cave.

The final secret to Aleut mummification was their choice of warm, dry caves for placing the bodies. The Aleutian Islands are noted for their volcanic activity. Subsurface heat escaping through cracks to the surface in the chosen caves insured that the mummies had optimal conditions for preservation. Burial caves with these characteristics have been found in several locations. Although the practice of mummification is ancient and continued even after early contact with Europeans, it has now been abandoned.

on end, then retired without saying a word to anyone. If animosity developed, men duelled verbally. Each man had to listen to his antagonist without showing anger. When near the end of life, some Aleut men went out in their kayaks never to return again. Women tirelessly worked on clothing and baskets for hours at a time. All respected the actions of others and were careful not to offend or insult. Positive reinforcement rather than punishment maintained harmony in Aleut communities. In the 18th century, a violent group of men, driven by the ruthless quest for profits at any cost, descended on the Aleuts, and their coming eventually resulted in the destruction of this unique system of cultural adaptations.

Contact and experience with Europeans

In 1741, the Danish explorer Vitus Bering, in the employ of the Russian government, made the first European landing in Alaska. The discovery of millions of sea otter quickly prompted commercial efforts by independent fur trappers and traders of Cossack descent known as *promyshlenniki*. They sought furs and used a variety of techniques from trade to theft to their ultimate technique, taking wives hostage in order to coerce Aleut men into hunting for them. The Aleuts fought back and were able to inflict several defeats on the invaders. By the late 1780s, however, effective Aleut resistance had been broken and the Russians subjugated them. The tremendous skill of the Aleut men as open-ocean hunters was irreplaceable. They were quickly incorporated as the backbone of the Russian-American Company, a monopoly authorized by the Czar in 1790 to control activities in Alaska. Aleut men were taken from their ancestral homes as far as the Santa Catalina Islands off southern California and forced to hunt sea otters and fur seals for the Russians.

In 1786, the Russians discovered the Pribilof Islands. The two main islands, Saint Paul and Saint George, are the major fur seal breeding grounds in the North Pacific. The Russians forcibly relocated a group of Aleut to harvest the seals; descendants of those first Aleuts continue to occupy the Pribilof Islands to this day.

The combination of warfare, disease and starvation wiped out entire villages, reducing the Aleut people to less than 20 percent of the precontact level. In the 19th century, the Russian government tightened control over the commercial activities of the Russian-American Company and sent Russian Orthodox priests to Alaska. Although they established hospitals, schools, and created an Aleut *orthography* (writing system), it was far too little too late for the devastated Aleuts to recover.

21

Arthur Eide, photographer, noted that this Eskimo living near Pt. Barrow "lost his leg in the ice, made his crutches and does as well as anyone." Photo circa 1910. Inupiat elders who could no longer assist in producing necessities were known to commit suicide by leaving the group in times of stress so that others could survive.

North Alaska Coast People
(Tareumiut)

Point Hope

Ko

Seward Peninsula

Nome

Bering Straits People

Yu

N

Barrow

Interior North Alaska Coast
People (Nunamiut)

River

ue Sound
eople

River

The blanket toss was
traditionally held following
the conclusion of a successful
whale hunt. The "blanket"
was traditionally made from
seal skins. Jumpers vied to
see whose acrobatics could
impress the onlookers the
most. Note the seal bladder
used as a prop.

lorthern Eskimos:
Inupiat

CHAPTER 3

Northern Eskimos: Inupiat

For most people, Alaska is the home of the Eskimo — hardy, ruddy-faced Natives who live in isolated igloos, wear warm fur clothing, use dogs and sleds to constantly travel in pursuit of polar bear while barely surviving on the edge of starvation.

As with any stereotype, there is a kernel of truth to this image but only a very small one. That kernel consists of hardy, fur clothes, dogs and sleds. After that, serious revisions are in order. For the north Alaskan Eskimos (Inupiat), there were no igloos (except in extreme emergencies); many lived nearly year round in the largest Alaskan Native communities at the time of contact; seal, bowhead whale, caribou and fish were their main foods, and starvation, although not unknown, was rare.

The Inupiat, which means "the people" in the Inupiaq language, can be divided into four main units: Bering Straits people, Kotzebue Sound people, North Alaska Coast people and Interior North Alaska people (Damas, 1985). The latter two groups have sometimes been termed the *Tareumiut* (people of the sea) and *Nunamiut* (people of the land). These regional groupings are based on patterns of social interaction between groups that arose out of proximity, intermarriage and kinship.

The Inupiat recognized smaller units which might be termed bands that consisted of closely related families of between 20 and 200 people who occupied and used a certain area. Each of these units had the suffix *miut* which means "people of." The larger coastal communities such as Wales, Pt. Hope and Barrow with 400–600 people actually consisted of a number of extended family units.

Population distribution

The population of the Inupiat is estimated to have been a around 10,000 people at the time of contact with Euroamericans in the 19th century.

**Inupiat Eskimo Groups and Estimated Population
at the Time of Contact**

Bering Straits	2,250
Kotzebue Sound	4,000
Interior North Alaska	1,500
North Alaska Coast	1,850
TOTAL	9,600

Food and diet

Three major ways of surviving were pursued by the Inupiat at the time of contact indicating their ability to adjust to different circumstances. These were large marine mammal hunting, mixed hunting and fishing, and caribou hunting.

The North Alaska Inupiat and the Bering Straits Inupiat of Wales, King Island, Sledge Island and Diomede Island depended heavily on large marine mammals such as bowhead whales, beluga whales and walrus. The Inupiat pursued these species when they migrated north in the late spring and summer. If the hunt was successful, they would not have to spend long hours on the winter ice, fishing or hunting seal.

Kotzebue Sound people and the remainder of the Bering Straits people harvested small sea mammals, land mammals, fish and migratory waterfowl. Pink and chum salmon were available to many groups in Norton and Kotzebue sounds. Other fish such as inconnu and whitefish were also important to virtually all groups. Herring and crab were used by the people of Norton Sound. Seals were a critical resource to all coastal groups while groups in the river valleys used caribou. Caribou provided about 90 percent of the Nunamiut diet (Hall 1985). During the spring and fall migrations, caribou herds would mass together making it easier to kill large numbers. People took a variety of other foods including mountain sheep, whitefish, hares, moose, bear, ground squirrel and ptarmigan.

Tools and technology

Eskimos are rightfully regarded as ingenious technologists whose inventions made it possible to survive the harsh living conditions of the arctic. The Inupiat tool kit consisted of a variety of stone and ivory tools made for butchering, tanning, carving, drilling, inscribing, sharpening and flaking. One of the most important tools was the bow drill, used for starting fires and drilling holes in wood, bone and ivory. With this relatively simple tool kit, the entire technological inventory could be made.

25

The Tareumiut, or "people of the sea," developed ingenious tools and methods for hunting seals, whales and other marine mammals. During the late 19th century, their resourcefulness and generosity saved many Yankee whalers whose vessels were trapped in the grip of the Arctic ice.

The most sophisticated technology was developed for the bowhead whale hunt and included *toggle-headed harpoons*, lances and lines. Floats made from seal bladders had special plugs for inflation. Other implements included scratching boards for attracting seals to breathing holes, bows, arrows, spears, spear throwers, bolas for taking birds, and a variety of snares. Fishing gear included nets, traps made of branches and roots, spears and hooks. The Nunamiut constructed long funnel-shaped rock and wood fences to divert caribou into lakes or a corral where waiting hunters would kill them.

Transportation

Another key item in the successful adaptation of the coastal peoples was the *umiak*, or large open skin boat. Most boats were 15–20 feet long, but Burch (1985) reports some nearly 50 feet from the Kotzebue area. Six to eight bearded seal skins were stitched together and carefully lashed to a wooden frame. Umiaks were used for hunting whales and walrus, and for travel and trading voyages. Large models could carry up to 15 people and a ton of cargo comfortably.

Better known is the *kayak*, or closed skin boat, used typically by one man among Eskimo groups. These were constructed by attaching stitched seal skins to wooden frames leaving only a circular opening in the top for entry.

For travel on land, the basket sled was used for general transport and the flat sled for hauling the large skin boats across the ice to the sea. Dogs were not used with sleds until after 1500 A.D. Snowshoes were used in interior regions with deeper snow fall such as the Kobuk River valley.

Clothing and decoration

Special clothing designs were developed to overcome the severe Arctic living conditions. Men's and women's clothing consisted of outer and inner pullover tops, (the outer being called *parkas* or *kuspuks*), outer and inner pants, socks and boots. Tops and pants were made of caribou skin; the fur faced inward on the inner garments and outward on the outer garments. Hoods with drawstrings were attached to the pullover tops which varied in length from mid-thigh to knee length. The woman's pullover had a larger hood for carrying small children. Pants, both inner and outer, went from the waist to the knee or ankle and were stuffed into boots which came up to just below the knee. Skin socks were worn and boots (*kamiks*) were constructed in a variety of fashions and materials in order to meet different weather conditions. Gloves were made from various skins with the fur turned inside; usually they were connected with a leather strip which ran around the neck for quick, sure retrieval if it was necessary to take them off. Sea-mammal intestines were sown together to create waterproof outergarments in the Norton Sound area for fishing and kayaking.

Eskimo clothing was eminently suited for cold weather. The bulky, layered garments provided for maximum insulation from the air trapped between them. The drawstrings allowed ventilation to prevent under garments from becoming damp from sweat.

House types

The design of Eskimo houses was also well-suited for the Arctic. Although a variety of internal designs and materials were found in the Inupiat area, two key features were common. The first is the underground tunnel entrance which was constructed *below* the level of the living area within the house itself. This passage served as a cold trap insuring that cold air would not enter the living area. The second feature was that houses were semi-subterranean, capitalizing on the ground as insulation against winter wind and cold. In most areas, the distinctive seal-oil lamp, made from soapstone or pottery, was used for light and warmth. This shallow dish-like object used a moss wick for burning seal oil.

Sod blocks, sometimes laid over driftwood or whale-bone frames, were the basic materials for Inupiat house construction. Houses were generally dome-shaped. A gut-covered opening let in what little winter light was available and was uncovered for a smoke hole. The Inupiat house was rectangular, about 12–15 feet long and eight to ten feet wide and normally housed 8–12 people comfortably. The entry way opened onto a general living area with floors made from driftwood planks or whale bone. People slept against the back wall on a raised wooden platform covered with polar bear and caribou skins.

Equipment and food was stored either below the house in a food cellar or in compartments in the entry tunnel.

In summer, many of these houses became flooded when the ground thawed. This was not a great problem since most people left for different seasonal camps to hunt and fish.

Inupiat communities also had *qargis* or *kashims* which served as men's houses or community houses. They were constructed by an extended family under the leadership of an elder male. The qargi was used primarily as a work area to make tools and repair equipment but also were ceremonial centers for dancing and feasting in the winter.

Trade   Trade was an important aspect of Inupiat life, particularly after establishment of Russian outposts in Siberia in the late 17th century made tobacco and other European goods available through exchange with the Chukchi. More traditional trade, such as that carried out in the trading partnerships, brought interior and coastal peoples together for the exchange of products. Seal oil and *muktuk* (whale skin) were prized by interior peoples who provided caribou and other fur skins in exchange for them. Trade fairs, attended by people from many areas, were conducted in the mid-summer at several locations.

Social organization   Kinship was the most important principle of Inupiat society. Among most groups, strangers were treated as dangerous enemies who could be killed unless they could establish some kinship relationship with a member of the group into whose territory they entered. As in modern American society, Inupiat reckoned kinsmen *bilaterally*—that is relatives on both the mother's and father's sides were equally important. In fact anthropologists label a kinship system which uses the same terms for relatives on either side (i.e. uncle, aunt, grandmother, grandfather, cousin) an "Eskimo" kinship system. In such a system, each individual has a *kindred*, a group of related individuals drawn equally from parents, siblings and their offspring on both mother's and father's sides. These would be the people that would occupy a home or homes close together and with whom most activities would be conducted.

Given the danger of not being related, a variety of mechanisms were developed in Inupiat society for establishing quasi-kinship relationships. One of these was the trading partnership which was used to link together men from different groups who could then exchange goods. These longstanding relationships could include short-term exchange of spouses as part of the generosity between the two families. Inupiat who had the same name also recognized a relationship between each other. Finally, adoption was quite common and also served to establish a special relationship between people.

Eskimo society has long been considered a model of egalitarianism in which all men were equal and judged solely by their achievements. Among the Inupiat, this stereotype must be seriously qualified. Although slavery and rigid classes did not exist, there was considerable property and wealth to be inherited in the form of boats and hunting equipment. The *umialik*, literally "captain of the umiak," was a substantial figure, responsible for many activities including the whale hunt, the qargi, ceremonies, festivals, religious rituals and trading expeditions.

Umiaks could be used for many purposes other than travel. This one is helping to dry laundry. When overturned, they could provide emergency shelter from storms which develop quickly in the Bering Sea.

This unique and multifaceted role had both achieved and ascribed elements as powerful and successful whale hunters could attract a following from beyond their kinsmen. However, those who inherited whaling equipment and training had a head start in attaining umialik status.

Male and female roles were complementary but strictly divided and hierarchical; males were dominant. Preferential female infanticide was practiced, but due to the many accidental deaths suffered by males, the number of men and women tended to be fairly balanced.

Women were trained in the skills of tanning, sewing and food preparation; wives observed many taboos and rituals to assist their husbands' hunting. These included a broad range of activities such as cutting skins at certain times, eating certain foods or looking in certain directions. It was thought that if those taboos were broken, then bad luck would befall the husband's hunting efforts.

Another stereotype about Eskimos is that they are cheerful, friendly and open. Burch, however, suggests that there was a high degree of competitiveness evident in Inupiat society and that stress was placed on competence as well as being better than one's peers. Certainly one of the great pastimes of the Inupiat was engaging in a wide variety of

Eskimo women and children, Teller, 1906.

The Frozen Family of Utqiagvik

During the early morning hours of a winter night between 125 and 400 years ago, an *ivu*, a huge block of shorefast ice, toppled onto a house at Utqiagvik, near present day Barrow. The sod covered wooden frame collapsed and crushed to death five occupants of the house. There were four females aged 42, 25, 15 and 8½ and one male aged 20 sleeping in the house at the time. Both of the older females had recently given birth and the 42-year old had been nursing at the time of her death. Neither infant nor husband, however, were found. We know that the roof collapsed in the early morning because the occupants had empty stomachs but full bladders.

The frozen family probably consisted of two related families. The 25-year old woman is thought to have been the eldest daughter of the 42-year old. Analysis of the male tool kits in the house revealed two different sets of property marks used by men to distinguish their harpoon points. One set of marks is still used by Point Hope hunters today. The younger woman's husband likely was living with his wife's family after their marriage which Inupiat elders indicate would have been a standard cultural practice.

The autoposy of the two older women revealed interesting information about their health. Lines on leg bones indicate that periods of food shortage, probably in late winter, occurred every three to five years. The older woman suffered from a heart infection, artherosclerosis and had experienced pneumonia. Many of her teeth were gone and those which remained showed heavy evidence of wear. Both women suffered from osteoporosis, softening of the bones, probably due to a lack of vitamin D in the diet. Both also suffered from severely blackened lungs due to the soot given off from the seal oil lamp. This was probably exacerbated by sleeping by the lamp and tending it through the night.

The Inupiat elders have returned the frozen family to their graves, but the misfortune of those ancients has resulted in fascinating scientific findings concerning life in the high arctic several centuries ago.

Gambling was a favorite pastime of many Native men. These Inupiat men are gambling for walrus tusks in the shadow of an umiak.

competitive games which tested the strength, stamina and pain thresholds of the participants.

Perhaps another indicator of the competitiveness of Inupiat society is the frequency of intersocietal warfare. Particularly for Bering Straits and Kotzebue Sound people, territorial boundaries were well-known and defended from interlopers. Both engaged in serious conflict with the Chukchi and Siberian Eskimo even though they also traded with them.

Within the local group, tensions between men could be controlled through the *song duel*. In this event, a man who felt wronged by another would challenge him to an exchange of belittling songs. The entire group would gather to witness the duel. The men would take turns singing songs which through wit and derision identified the wrongdoing or falsity of the other person. The group would respond with laughter to each song and the duel would continue until one man withdrew in shame. The matter was expected to be closed with the ending of the duel.

Ceremonies

Several ceremonies were important to the Inupiat. Among all groups, the *Messenger Feast*, the practice of inviting a group from another area to one's home community, was common. The feast occurred in the fall or winter and was sponsored by an umialik who invited his partner from another group. The visitors were presented gifts when they arrived followed by several days of dances, feasts and games.

Several additional special ceremonies were conducted by the North Alaska Coastal Inupiat to whom the bowhead whale hunt was critical. In the spring, a preparatory feast was held in which umialiks distributed all the remaining whale meat from the previous year which had not yet been eaten. This was to meet the requirement that one should only take when one was in need and was a means of displaying the people's worthiness to the whale. New clothes and equipment were brought out because this was a festival of renewal, of insuring the continuation of life.

If the whale hunt was successful, then a celebratory feast would be held after the whaling in the early summer. This was called the *Nalukataq*, when the famous blanket toss was held. For the blanket toss, a large blanket made from several seal skins sewn together was held in a large circle by a group of people. One person at a time would get on the blanket and be tossed skyward to songs and chants. Cheers would be given to those who were the most acrobatic in their airborne maneuvers.

Beliefs The Inupiat belief system appears to have been based on the principle of reincarnation and the recycling of spirit forms from one life to the next. This was was true of both the human and animal worlds. Names of those who had recently died would be given to newborn infants. Animal spirits were seen as critical for only if they were released could the animal be regenerated and return for future human harvest. Consequently, a great number of special behaviors were accorded various animals including offering marine mammals a drink of freshwater, cutting the throats or skull to release the spirit, and taking care to make maximum use of the products. If the special behaviors were not faithfully carried, the animals might not make themselves available again. Shamans had a special place in Inupiat society as curers and forecasters of weather and future events.

Contact with Europeans The isolation of the Inupiat made them one of the last groups of Alaskan Natives to encounter Europeans and Americans. Several voyages of exploration made incidental contact in the early 19th century. But it was not until the Yankee whalers followed the bowhead whale through the Bering Straits in the 1850s, that the era of sustained and substantial interaction with Euroamericans began for the Inupiat.

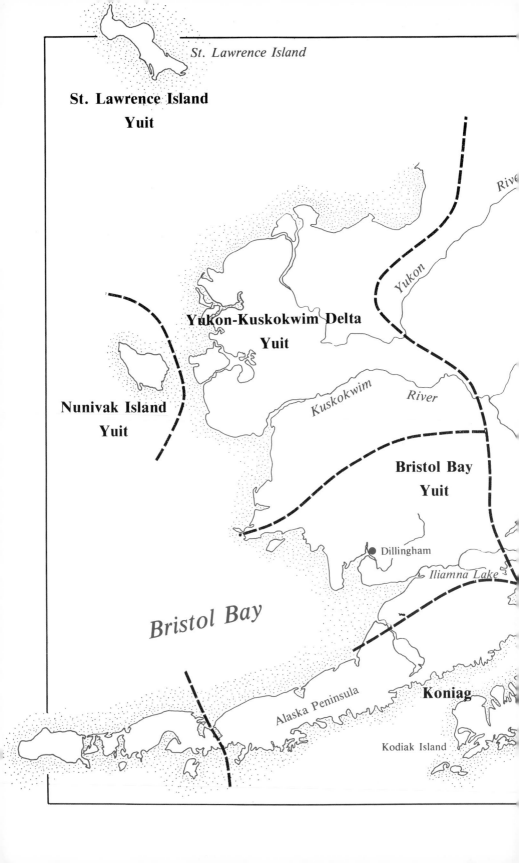

St. Lawrence Island

**St. Lawrence Island
Yuit**

River

**Yukon-Kuskokwim Delta
Yuit**

Yukon

**Nunivak Island
Yuit**

Kuskokwim   River

**Bristol Bay
Yuit**

● Dillingham

Iliamna Lake

Bristol Bay

Koniag

Alaska Peninsula

Kodiak Island

Among the Yuit, young boys entered the men's house when they were about ten years old. Here they learned the hunting and tool making skills they would need as adults. Photo taken in Teller about 1905.

Anchorage

Valdez

Chugach

Eyak

uit

Gulf of Alaska

N

outhern Eskimos:
Yuit

CHAPTER 4

Southern Eskimos: Yuit

The most diverse group of Alaskan Natives are the southern Eskimos or Yuit, speakers of the Yup'ik languages. At the time of contact, they were the most numerous of the Alaska Native groups. Communities stretched from Prince William Sound on the north Pacific Coast to St. Lawrence Island in the central Bering Sea. The Yuit settled this vast region from west to east reaching the Kodiak archipelago and Prince William Sound by about 2,000 years ago.

The Yuit are usually divided into Bering Sea groups and Pacific groups. This classification is based on technological, subsistence and language differences. In the Bering Sea group, the major language spoken is Central Yup'ik. St. Lawrence Island Yup'ik is a separate language. The Pacific Eskimos all speak dialects of Alutiiq, another Yup'ik language.

The most meaningful social unit was a named group of closely related extended families with a common territory. This grouping was designated by the suffix "miut." Early historic accounts are unclear on the number of such named groups. According to Van Stone (1984), the Bering Sea Yuit, exclusive of the St. Lawrence Island people, were divided into seven major groups plus additional smaller groups. St. Lawrence Island people were also divided into an unknown number of small, local village groups prior to contact.

In the Pacific Eskimo region, basically three large groupings are recognized: the Koniag, who occupied the Kodiak archipelago and the southside of the Alaska Peninsula; the Chugach, who occupied Prince William Sound; and the little known Unegkurmiut on the south coast of the Kenai Peninsula. Both the Chugach and Koniag were subdivided into a number of smaller local groups.

In general, between 100–300 people could be found living in sedentary villages in protected locations during the winter. In the spring, family or extended family groups dispersed to various camps to obtain migratory waterfowl, salmon, caribou and other resources. Substantial movements of people throughout the spring, summer and fall was necessary to insure that adequate resources would be acquired before the winter.

Population distribution   The total population of Alaskan Yup'ik speaking peoples was approximately 30,000 at the time of contact.

**Yuit Eskimo Groups and Estimated Population
at the Time of Contact**

Bering Sea Yuit	
St. Lawrence Island	1,500
Nunivak Island	500
Yukon-Kuskokwim Delta	13,000
Bristol Bay	3,000
Subtotal	18,000
Pacific Yuit	
Alaska Peninsula	500
Kodiak Archipelago	8,000
Kenai Peninsula	250
Prince William Sound	3,500
Subtotal	12,350
Yuit Total	30,350

Food and diet   In the Bering Sea division, several different adaptations were practiced. The St. Lawrence Islanders depended on walrus for their main food supply and many materials; the people's lifestyle closely resembled that of the Inupiat large marine mammal hunters. Bowhead whales and seals were also used but were of secondary importance.

On the mainland from the lower part of Norton Sound to Bristol Bay, several different subsistence strategies are evident. In the lower reaches of the major salmon producing rivers such as the Yukon, Kuskokwim, Togiak, Nushagak and Kvichak, intensive salmon fishing was dominant with other fish, seals, beluga whales and terrestrial mammals secondary. On the outer coast of the Yukon-Kuskokwim delta, seal and beluga hunting were primary and were combined with fishing for a variety of freshwater and saltwater species and hunting small terrestrial mammals. Away from the coast and major river valleys, salmon fishing was combined with hunting larger terrestrial mammals, particularly caribou. Throughout the mainland area, migratory waterfowl and their eggs were a crucial early spring resource and a variety of greens, roots and berries were also collected and stored for winter use.

Pacific Yuit subsistence was heavily marine oriented. Whales, seals, salmon, halibut, cod and rockfish were major food sources. Sea lions, sea otters, porpoises, shellfish, sea

37

urchins, clams, chitons, blue mussels and seaweed all contributed to the diet. Deer on Kodiak Island and in Prince William Sound and caribou and moose on the Alaska Peninsula along with ground squirrels and hare were important supplementary food sources. Bear and mountain goat (among the Chugach) were occasionally taken. A variety of greens, roots and berries rounded out the Pacific Eskimo diet.

Transportation

The Yuit used several different methods of ocean travel. St. Lawrence Island Yuit hunted large marine mammals from open skin boats, 20 to 40 feet in length. Hughes (1985) suggests that kayaks, the closed, one-man vessels, might not have been used at all by St. Lawrence Islanders. Pacific Yuit, on the other hand, appear to have reversed the emphasis using the kayak or baidarka to a much greater extent than the umiak (Clark 1985).

This is a reflection of the different whaling strategies utilized by the two groups. Pacific Yuit used the same technique practiced by the Aleut, that of lancing the whale with aconite poison individually from kayaks, while the St. Lawrence Island groups utilized the cooperative effort based on harpoons, floats and lines deployed from umiaks.

Among the mainland Yuit, the kayak or baidarka was most important, although the umiak was also used, primarily for long-distance travel and trading. Kayaks were used for sealing and beluga hunting but also for tending drift and set gillnets. The nets were made from caribou skin or willow bark and were used for catching salmon in the larger rivers.

Platforms provided a location for storing food and supplies throughout the year. Note the two sleds and kayak frame.

House types   The Yuit constructed a wide variety of dwellings. Among the mainland Bering Sea Yuit, houses were rectangular structures, partially dugout, approximately 12 feet by 15 feet. Most had underground entry tunnels. Where wood was available, plank walls and house posts with wooden beams would be overlain with grass or bark. Otherwise, sod was used. The inside had an open work and cooking area with a central hearth at one end and a raised sleeping platform with furs at the other. Floors were generally dirt. The house was occupied by a group of related women and their children. Husbands and sons constructed the homes and then visited wives and mothers.

People on Kodiak Island also lived in semi-subterranean sod covered structures but used surface entry as opposed to a tunnel. A large central room and central hearth served as work area, living area and kitchen. Side rooms were used for sleeping and privacy. The rooms could also be used for steambaths which were made by pouring water over hot rocks. Steambaths were used for purification, relaxation, and social interaction and were enjoyed by both men and women. They continue to be a major pastime in many Bering Sea mainland Yuit villages to this day.

In Prince William Sound at the time of contact, the Chugach lived in planked wooden houses that reflected their forest surroundings and their contacts with the Tlingits further east. The house plan, however, retained the central area and side rooms characteristic of Koniag dwellings.

All Yuit communities, save the St. Lawrence Islanders, had additional larger structures (up to 30 feet by 30 feet), known as *kashgees* or *kashims*, sometimes called men's houses. Among the mainland Yuit these structures were lived in by a group of related males who worked, slept, ate and socialized together. Large open areas with planked floors served as working and living areas. One or two levels of platforms around the outside walls provided sleeping places. Tools and equipment were hung from the ceiling or placed under the platforms. The central hearth was covered to make a smooth floor during ceremonies. The kashgee also served as a steambath for the men.

Summer fish camps along major rivers had substantial wood and sod structures similar to those in the winter village. Less permanent structures such as tents and lean-tos were used in other areas.

Other structures were found around the outside of these dwellings including caches for storing food and equipment, racks for drying fish, storage pits, and frameworks for storing kayaks and umiaks.

39

Storyknife

Elsie was excited. In a little while she and her grandmother were going down to the river. Besides fetching water, the trip to the river meant that grandmother would tell her a story accompanied by pictures which grandmother would draw in the mud bank.

This unique form of teaching culture to the young, called *storyknife*, was practiced by mainland Yuit grandmothers with their granddaughters. A small (4 to 10 inch), scimitar-shaped dull knife was used to draw pictures on a muddy, flat surface such as the bank of a river. These illustrations accompanied stories through which the grandmother entertained and taught the child. The knives were usually carved by a young girl's father and given to the daughter at a community ceremony. Standardized symbols were developed in different villages to represent houses, adult males and females, infants, and activities such as walking, eating and sewing.

Elderly Yuit women recount that the stories they were told in their youth had important information about domestic activities (sewing, cooking, weaving) and appropriate behaviors (respect for elders, quiet, avoidance of dangerous areas) and about what would happen if they engaged in inappropriate behavior. A common theme was the grandmother telling the young girl what not to do, the young girl doing it and then something dreadful (usually death) happening to the grandmother. This training emphasized obedience, the interdependence of people and the responsibility of a person for his actions.

As missionaries and schools in western Alaska assumed the role of educator, the activity shifted to creative storytelling between young girls rather than teaching from grandmother to granddaughter. Although some of the older stories and themes about behaviors and values continued, new stories of a make-believe kind and scary stories concerning monsters entered the repetoires. Storyknife continues down to the present day as a form of play and teaching values in some villages but the competition from television and school may ultimately result in the disappearance of this colorful and useful activity.

Clothing and decoration

Clothing varied depending on the environment. St. Lawrence Islanders wore distinctive reindeer skin, hooded pullover parkas similar to those of the North Alaskan Inupiat. Waterproof parkas were made from walrus intestines while sealskins provided the materials for boots and mittens. Bering Sea mainland Yuit wore a wide variety of garments made of skins from seal, caribou, birds and salmon. They were similar but generally longer and looser fitting than Inupiat garments. Waterproof boots constructed from salmon skins were distinctive. Pacific Eskimos garb emphasized waterproof overgarments with little use of boots or trousers.

Koniag wore wooden visors similar to those of the Aleuts. In Prince William Sound, circular spruce root hats were adopted by the Chugach from the Tlingit.

Other components of personal adornment also varied. Labrets were common among all Yuit. Nose and ear piercing were common among Pacific Eskimos. St. Lawrence Island males wore distinctive tonsured hair styles in which the top portion of the head was shaved while a 2–3 inch long circle of hair immediately above the forehead was retained. Women wore their hair long either braided or down. Three parallel straight tatoo lines from just below the bottom lip to the chin were common among the women. Among the Chugach and Koniag, this signified that a woman had reached puberty.

The Yuit enjoyed the bounty of some of the world's richest salmon fisheries. Large quantities of fish were harvested and processed through relentless hours of work in order to sustain families and their dogs throughout the long winters.

NATIVES DRYING SALMON

41

Social organization   The Yuit organized their social relationships in a variety of different ways. On St. Lawrence Island patrilineal descent groups which Hughes (1984) terms *clans* were important to residence and participation in a wide variety of subsistence and ceremonial activities. Patrilineally related males comprised the marine mammal hunting crews and organized rituals in preparation for the hunt. Houses were owned and occupied by a group of patrilineally related males, their wives and children. Women married into these clans, and there was a formal process of gift exchange and brideservice where the groom worked for his in-laws for a period of time before the woman took up residence in her husband's house.

Elsewhere, among mainland Bering Sea and Pacific Yuit, it appears that descent is nominally matrilineal. Nevertheless, relatives on either side were central to the daily relationships and activities of an individual. Women owned the smaller domiciles in the Bering Sea mainland communities and delivered food to the kashims which were occupied and owned by a group of matrilineally related men. The descent system used by the Koniag and Chugach probably was matrilineal.

The Pacific Eskimo recognized social status distinctions in their society. Leaders of villages were considered to have high status and the positions were inherited. Slaves were also taken.

Among the Bering Sea mainland Yuit, social distinctions were less apparent. Although there were leaders who coordinated the construction and use of kashgees and accumulated and distributed wealth, the position was not hereditary and there do not appear to have been slaves in the society. Leadership was of a kin group or kashim and not of a village.

St. Lawrence Island Yuit recognized a leadership position of the patrilineal clan for purposes of coordinating the whale hunt, conducting the appropriate rituals, and constructing and owning houses. Communities normally consisted of closely related families so the group leader was also the village leader. When several patrilineal kin groups occupied a single village, no village leader was recognized. The position of clan leader was apparently largely achieved; slavery was not practiced on St. Lawrence Island.

Bering Sea Yuit groups recognized important social relationships beyond those of close kinship. The most important of these was the "partnership" relationship established between men which usually constituted a lifetime commitment to assist and share a variety of activities with each other.

Since this relationship could be between men of the same community, it was not necessarily motivated by reciprocal trading as among the Inupiat.

Beliefs

Yuit religious belief systems were heavily influenced by two basic notions. The first of these was that human success in hunting depended on maintaining a positive relationship between people and the spirits of the animals hunted. Amulets, taboos and other ritual activities were designed to show respect to those animal spirits in order to ensure continued availability. The second principle was that of reincarnation or the cycling of life. It was believed that human spirits were recycled into life through birth and naming. Those who had not been reborn lived in the underground but occasionally could appear above ground. It was necessary to be vigilant and not to offend these spirits since they could bring harm.

The Yuit world was inhabited by many spirits including those of the deceased. Spirit poles were erected by graves to keep the spirits of the dead from disrupting the world of the living. *("Memorials to the Dead, Kuskokwim River," from the Weinland Collection, Henry E. Huntington Library.)*

Ceremonies

The ceremonial systems of both the Bering Sea and Pacific Yuit were elaborate although there were substantial differences. They combined elements of the religious belief system with important principles of social interaction and control. They also provide evidence of the restraint, balance and reciprocity which are central themes to Yuit culture. Among St. Lawrence Islanders, a series of ritual ceremonies preceded the whale hunting season in order to purify the hunters and placate the whale. This involved offerings to the whale and consumption of all food from previous harvests. Following a successful hunt, the captain's wife offered welcome and a drink of water to the captured whale as among the northern coastal Inupiat followed by a feast and ceremony of thanks. The men could not return to hunting until five days later. At the conclusion of the whaling season, a large community-wide celebration was held.

The Bering Sea mainland Yuit are considered to have the most complex ceremonial system of any Eskimo group. The ceremonial season was named *cauyaq* after the circular drum made by stretching seal gut over a wooden frame. These ceremonies were normally conducted in the winter and early spring and varied from four to seven days depending on the group. Elaborate masks of wood with attached symbols representing spirits were an important element in the dancing that was central to the ceremonies. One major ceremony found virtually everywhere was the so-called *Messenger's Feast* in which two villages of closely related people took turns in hosting a large celebration of feasting, dancing, and gift distribution. The name came from the practice of sending a formal messenger to a village to present the invitation and indicate what special products the invitees should bring. These events were conducted at the village level (as opposed

Masks representing animal and other spirits were an important part of religious ceremonies and dances.

to the kashgee level as among the Inupiat) and with an aura of friendly competition. Among certain groups, social control mechanisms were built into Messenger Feasts by collecting embarrassing instances of social transgressions by members of the invited village and poking fun at them through dances. This indicated to all present what the norms of the group were and the shame that could befall those who violated them.

Another important feast was the *Bladder Feast* through which the mainland Bering Sea Yuit demonstrated their respect for the seal and sought to insure that seal populations would be abundant. During the course of a year, bladders from all the seals taken were saved, dried out and hung up in the kashgee. In the winter, after new clothes and equipment for the coming season were manufactured, preparations were made for the five day bladder festival. The seal bladders were taken down and inflated. Since it was believed that the seal spirits would return at that time to the vicinity of the kashgee to witness the ceremony, noise was kept at a minimum in order not to disturb the seal spirits.

The key element of the ritual was the belief that the seal spirit or life force was housed in the bladder. By killing the seal when it was awake, the seal's spirit would be able to return in another body if the bladder were returned to the seal's home under the sea. After five days of dancing, the people took down the inflated bladders, marched to the nearby river, cut a hole through the ice and returned the bladders to the sea. The spirits of the seals could then return to their home underneath the sea and be reborn. The *angulcaq* (shaman) had a special role for he was to leave the festival and travel to the home of the seals to see if they had been satisfied with the human efforts. After several days, the angulcaq returned with the good news. The seals were happy and would be returning in abundance. Through this ceremony the Yuit demonstrated the mutual dependence of men upon seals and seals upon men for the recreation of life.

Contact with Europeans   Contact with Europeans and Americans occurred at radically different times for Yuit people depending on where they lived. The Koniag and Chugach fell under the brutal transformative influence of the Russians in the 1780s, resulting in substantial population decline. The St. Lawrence Island Yuit were not seriously impacted until the coming of the Yankee whalers in the 1850s. Mainland Bering Sea Yuit have been able to maintain their culture, language and communities to a greater extent than other Alaska Native groups due to the lack of major European or American influence on them until well into the 20th century.

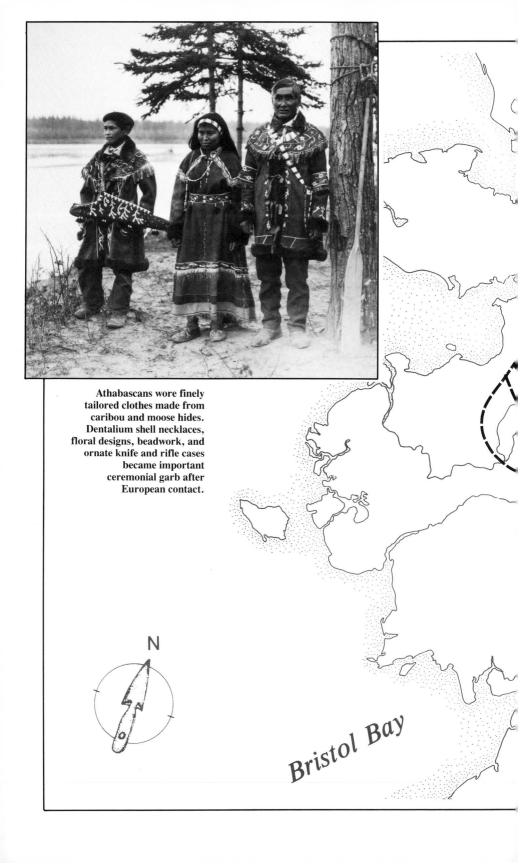

Athabascans wore finely tailored clothes made from caribou and moose hides. Dentalium shell necklaces, floral designs, beadwork, and ornate knife and rifle cases became important ceremonial garb after European contact.

N

Bristol Bay

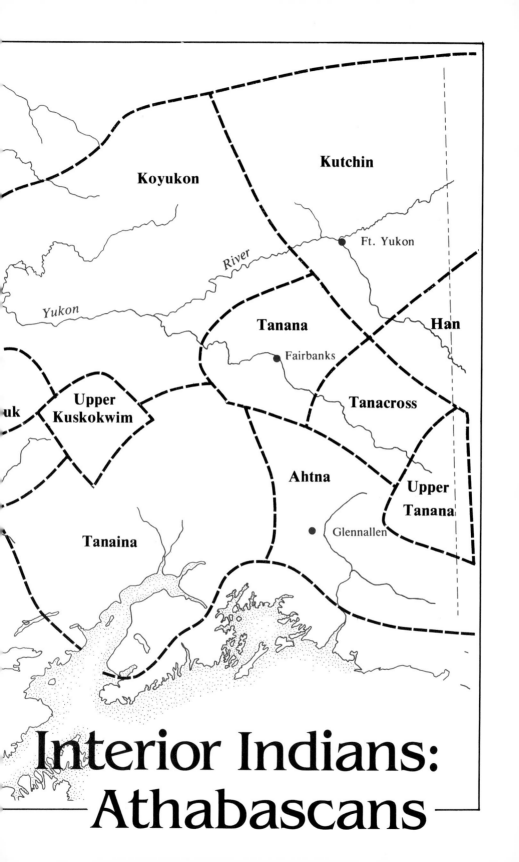

Koyukon

Kutchin

• Ft. Yukon

River

Yukon

Tanana

Han

• Fairbanks

uk

Upper
Kuskokwim

Tanacross

Ahtna

Upper
Tanana

Tanaina

• Glennallen

Interior Indians:
Athabascans

CHAPTER 5

Interior Indians: Athabascans

Athabascan Indians occupy the broad interior of Alaska between the Brooks Range on the north and the Alaska Range on the south as well as the Copper and Susitna river valleys which drain southward from the Alaska Range. The only Athabascan group to live by the ocean were the Tanaina who resided along the shores of Cook Inlet. Alaskan Athabascan speakers are closely related to northern Canadian Athabascan speakers of the Yukon Territory, Northwest Territories and British Columbia and also to the Navajo and Apache of the American southwest.

There are nine Athabascan ethnic-linguistic groupings in Alaska. Characteristics of these groups include similar language, endogamy (marriage within the group), ceremonies and beliefs. Each of the nine ethnic groups are subdivided into units termed regional bands, and in most cases they are further subdivided into local bands consisting of between 15–75 people in several related families. Local bands were generally led by men who had demonstrated special competence in hunting, trading or organizing. Below the local band level was the household level of organization which consisted of one to three families sharing the same dwelling and basic daily activities. Among the more sedentary groups such as the Ingalik, Ahtna and Tanaina, the village was a recognized unit with a territory and chief.

Athabascans are considered flexible and adaptive people who incorporate implements, social principles and ceremonial practices from their non-Athabascan neighbors. Examples include the Tanaina use of the kayak, adapted from their Koniag and Chugach neighbors, the Ingalik use of the kashim adapted from their Yup'ik neighbors, and the Ahtna large plank dwellings, probably adopted from their Tlingit neighbors.

Archeological record

Athabascans developed the cache to keep food and supplies safe from their dogs and wild animals. The cache is a distinctive Alaska symbol and is still in use today. Photo taken near Copper River, 1910.

The archeological record from the interior of Alaska is one of great continuity and little change from 6000 years ago to about 1000 years ago. Sites have few artifacts and there is little evidence of wealth, ceremonial items or substantial population concentrations other than in major river valleys where salmon were available. The tools include large projectile points used with spears and small blades used with bows and arrows. In areas bordering Yuit populations in southern and southwest Alaska, interior sites show influence of that contact in the form of ulus, pottery and ground slate tools.

Population distribution

The total population of Alaskan Athabascans is estimated to have been 10–11,000 people at the time of contact. They were relatively sparsely distributed and were most numerous in areas where abundant runs of salmon provided a relatively stable food supply. They can be divided into riverine, upland and Pacific subdivisions based on their location and their basic hunting, fishing and gathering methods. Riverine groups occupied areas with good salmon fishing, upland groups depended on caribou and Pacific groups took advantage of salmon and other coastal resources.

Athabascan Groups and Estimated Population at the Time of Contact

Group	Population	Location
Riverine		
Ingalik	1500	Lower Yukon and Kuskokwim
Koyukon	2000	Middle Yukon and Koyukuk
Tanana	500	Lower Tanana
Holikachuk	500	Lower Middle Yukon and Innoko
Upland		
Kutchin	1500	Upper Yukon and Porcupine
Han	300	Upper Yukon
Upper Tanana	200	Upper Tanana
Pacific		
Ahtna	1000	Copper River
Tanaina	3000	Cook Inlet, Susitna and Upper Kuskokwim
TOTAL	10,500	

Food and diet   The subsistence strategies of Athabascan groups took two forms. Among the riverine and Pacific groups, salmon fishing was supplemented by fall moose and caribou hunting, as well as spring waterfowling and small mammal hunting. The upland groups who lacked access to substantial salmon runs hunted caribou intensively in the fall. They also hunted moose and small furbearers such as beaver, hare and ground squirrel and fished for whitefish, blackfish, pike and other freshwater species in the spring and winter. Berries, greens and roots were collected by all groups during the summer months.

Opportunities for hunting, fishing and gathering largely determined where Athabascans lived. Pacific and riverine groups were more sedentary, occupying substantial dwellings on the major rivers from November to March. During the summer and fall, the groups moved to as many as three different seasonal camps. All groups moved to summer fish camps to catch and dry salmon and most moved to fall upland camps for caribou drives. Riverine groups also moved to spring camps for muskrat, waterfowl and/or caribou hunting. A more nomadic existence was characteristic of the upland groups who had to pursue game and were not able to put up enough fish to last them through the winter.

House types   House types varied dramatically among Athabascans.

The Ingalik, heavily influenced by their Yuit neighbors, had semisubterranean log dwellings which had above ground entry ways. Villages consisted of 10–12 of these dwellings, each of which housed two families, plus a larger kashim.

The Koyukon and Tanana had semisubterranean log dwellings often built into the high banks of the Yukon and Tanana rivers.

The Tanaina constructed relatively large semisubterranean dwellings with a tunnel entry. Inside there was a large central room with a hearth and several side rooms. The walls were made of logs and banked with earth.

Among the Ahtna, a variety of houses were used including large plank houses which could accommodate up to ten families. These dwellings had an excavated central pit area with a hearth. Raised platforms next to the walls were divided with bark or bearskins into separate cubicles for families. The Ahtna also constructed a smaller house of bark laid over poles, similar to the dwelling constructed by their relatives, the Upper Tanana.

The Kutchin used a portable domeshaped caribou or moose skin tent constructed out of curved poles lashed together. The structure was about 14 feet in diameter and eight feet high. During the winter, it was heavily insulated with evergreen boughs and snow allowing the people relative comfort in some of the coldest temperatures on earth.

In the summer Athabascans used a variety of temporary constructions including tents, lean-tos and smaller versions of the winter lodges.

Athabascans were found living in a variety of house styles. Homes could be dugouts, plank houses or dome-shaped moose skin tents. This photo shows an Ahtna bark house.

Tools

Athabascan tools made from stone, bone and antler were used to modify skins and wood. Athabascans are distinctive among Alaska Natives for their use of bark, particularly that of the birch tree, for a variety of vessels, bowls, receptacles and containers.

Transportation

Riverine and upland groups traveled by birchbark canoes and mooseskin *coracles*, circular emergency vessels used for floating down rivers. Kayaks or baidarkas were used by the Tanaina.

Upland Athabascans were the masters of snowshoes, a variety of which were designed for different snow conditions.

Prior to contact, dogs were used essentially as pack animals and sleds were pulled by human power. Women assumed most of the burden of transporting goods from one place to another.

Athabascan food gathering techniques were limited but effective. A simple bow was the preferred hunting implement but a wide variety of snares and deadfalls trapped large and small game. Funnel-shaped fences were used to force caribou into corrals where they were killed. Basket traps, weirs, spears, nets and fishhooks were used to catch freshwater fish.

Birch bark canoes required skilled construction and were frequently repaired with patches and pitch. Smaller, easier to handle models were made for women. *(From the Charles Bunnell Collection, Alaska and Polar Regions Dept., University of Alaska-Fairbanks.)*

Dog Mushing

Dogs were domesticated in the New World about 10,000 years ago. Evidence has been found of their use in the arctic nearly 4,000 years ago. Dogs probably were first domesticated for warning and defense rather than for transportation or food. Archeological evidence based on harnesses, sled design and whips, indicates that dogs were not used for pulling sleds by Eskimos in Alaska until about 1500 A.D.

Interior Athabascans placed 35-pound saddlebags on their dogs to transport their belongings. However, the Kutchin and other Athabascans pulled their own sleds and toboggans.

In the postcontact period several factors combined to rapidly spread the use of dogs pulling sleds. The most important were the establishment of trading posts seeking furs and the introduction of the basket sled. By the late 19th century, dog teams transported supplies and equipment during the winter in most of northern, western and interior Alaska. This continued until the 1930s when airplanes began to displace dog teams.

The importance of dogs in the Athabascan trapping way of life led to an emphasis on small dogs built for speed and stamina. These dogs have come to be called Alaskan Huskies. Soon races in the villages emerged as men competed against each other to see who had the fastest team.

Huslia, a small Koyukon Athabascan village on the Koyukuk River, became the heart of dog racing in the 1940s, 1950s and 1960s. It produced a number of great mushers including Jimmy Huntington, Bobby Vent, and Cue Bifelt. But its most famous racing musher is George Attla, nicknamed the "Huslia Hustler" whose life story is told in the movie "Spirit of the Wind." Attla reached the pinnacle of his profession by overcoming a substantial leg injury. An uncompromising competitor, Attla also used modern methods of diet and selective breeding to maintain his team's position at the top of the sprint race profession in the 1980s. As long as there are dogs and young men in the villages of rural Alaska, racing with the wind like George Attla will remain a part of their lives.

Clothing and decoration

Clothing was unique in its tailored, form-fitting quality and was highly prized by other Native people. Among upland and riverine groups, standard men's garments consisted of a finely tanned white or light-colored caribou skin top which came to mid-thigh; among the Kutchin the garment dovetailed to a point in both front and back. Lower garments consisted of a single-piece legging combining pants and boots into a unified caribou skin garment. Women wore leggings and a pullover dress of tanned caribou skin which came to the knees. Winter garments retained the fur which was worn next to the body while summer garments were hairless.

Both men's and women's outer garments were decorated with a variety of geometric patterns made from porcupine quills, dentalium shells and seeds. Fringes were also a characteristic feature around the bottom of the women's dresses and men's tunics as well on the shoulders in the back. In winter hats and gloves made of beaver skin were common. Infants were carried in a bark cradleboard.

Additional personal adornment was limited among Athabascan groups. Dentalium shell necklaces, obtained through long-distance trade networks, were worn as symbols of wealth. Women might have three straight lines tatooed on their chins and men might have small linear tatoos on their arms symbolizing exploits in war. Nose pins were worn on festive occasions. Faces were painted with red being the preferred color among riverine groups.

Social organization

Athabascan social organization is a mixture of their own principles and practices adapted from neighboring groups. A fundamental Athabascan trait bases kinship on matrilineal descent. With the exception of the Ingalik and one group of Koyukon, all Athabascans had clans, named descent groups into which a person was born based on the mother's membership. In the riverine and upland groups, there were three such groupings which were exogamous (requiring spouses to be obtained from another clan). The Ahtna and Tanaina, who had 11 to 18 clans, also divided themselves into two matrilineal *moieties* (halves), known as Raven and Seagull. This is likely the result of contact with Tlingits who had similar principles of complex social organization.

Social stratification along wealth and class lines varied among Athabascans. All groups recognized and valued the efforts of individuals to acquire wealth because it would be redistributed through the potlatch. The wealthiest groups appear to have been the Tanaina, Ahtna and Ingalik. Among the Ahtna, a class of wealthy individuals might even be said to have existed. Slavery was practiced among a number of Athabascan groups, but was almost incidental, typically consisting of women or children captured in raids from other groups.

Most marriages were monogamous with women marrying in their mid-teens and men somewhat later. Wealthier males occasionally had several wives and, among the Kutchin, might use younger males to sire heirs by their younger wives. Among the Kutchin, high-status women occasionally had *polyandrous* (woman married to several men) unions to brothers (Slobodin 1984).

Good hunters, traders and organizers achieved leadership and attracted followers, usually through kinship principles. They had little formal authority, leading mostly by example and persuasion. Nevertheless, there were some exceptionally wealthy leaders.

The Koyukon, Kutchin and Tanaina were noted for warfare. The Kutchin fought steadily with the Koyukon and Inupiat while the Tanaina battled the Koniag, Chugach and occasionally the Ingalik. Tanaina villages were well hidden to protect them from attacks.

Athabascans generally lived in sparsely distributed groups but in places where large salmon runs occurred such as the Copper River (shown here), large groups congregated. Dip nets are still used today.

Trade was an important element in many Athabascan societies. The copper controlled by the Ahtna was highly valued by many groups and the Tanaina were noted traders between interior groups and the Koniag and Eskimo. The Koyukon and Kutchin traded with their Inupiat neighbors intensively after the 16th century.

Ceremonies

The major ceremonial event around which Athabascan society revolved was the *potlatch*. The term applies to various formal occasions when one group hosts another; gifts are distributed to the guests to mark important social events.

The most important potlatch was the mortuary feast given in honor of a deceased individual by his clan mates, usually a year or more after the death occurred. During the intervening period, close relatives manufactured and collected an abundance of blankets, other wealth items and food. At the appropriate time, an invitation was sent to other bands and clans to attend the potlatch. Upon arrival, the invitees received gifts in formal presentations followed by feasting and dancing. It was expected that the hosts later would be invited to a potlatch given by their guests. Gift giving was competitive with leaders vying to give more wealth and foods than their counterparts in other groups. The hosts were expected to give to destitution.

A particularly distinctive event developed by the Koyukon was the Stick Dance, a marathon circle dance conducted around a pole erected either in the center of the village or attached to the center of a building. This was part of the two day memorial celebration on behalf of a deceased individual. Participants were exhilarated, exhausted and uplifted by the emotional outpouring that characterized the marathon dance. It continues to be held from time to time among the Koyukon today.

Smaller potlatches were also given to celebrate events such as birth, marriage, a boys first successful hunt, and to rectify wrongs between groups such as accidents or insults.

A different but especially important event was the ritual associated with a young women's first menstruation. A separate hut was erected where the young girl would be sequestered for periods up to a year. A number of taboos were imposed and she was expected to stay away from contact with men and their hunting gear for fear of polluting it. She was attended by a kinswoman past menopause who taught her the skills and practices necessary for the adult female role. A special feast announced the completion of her ritual and her availability for marriage.

Beliefs   Athabascan beliefs about and relationships with the super-natural involved several important principles. A critical set of beliefs revolved around the indistinguishability between men and animals in the distant past. Both have spirits and in the past they communicated directly with each other. These ancient relationships had been transformed by the acts and antics of Raven, a culture hero and trickster who constantly disrupted the moral order by deception. The legend cycle told in stories to Athabascan children is composed of tales concerning the activities of Raven, along with other mythical beings which exemplify concepts of right and wrong in Athabascan culture.

Despite these transformations, important relationships between the spirits of men and animals continue. Especially important animals include the caribou, bear and wolf. Humans must remain respectful through ritual practices, such as sexual abstinence, and taboos in order to remain in the good graces of the animal spirits. Some individuals might obtain power through a special relationship with the spirit of an animal species.

Other malevolent spirits must not be offended. One of them, termed the "woodsman" or *nahani*, among contemporary Koyukon, lurks in the forest to capture children and is believed to be what people who are lost in the forest become.

An important intermediary with the spirits among the Pacific Athabascans was the shaman. Shamans acted as both magician and medical practitioner and could have either a good or bad reputation. Curing and predicting future events such as weather and hunting success were important activities of the shaman. Among the upland groups, shamans utilized *scapulimancy*, a method of divining the location of game when hunting success was limited. The scapula bone of a caribou was placed in a fire and the resulting cracks in the bone were interpreted by the shaman as indications of where the hunters should look for game.

Contact with Europeans   Direct contact with Russians, English, and Americans came relatively late to Athabascan groups due to their interior locations. In western Alaska, the effects of trade predated actual contact causing major shifts in village locations and the seasonal activities of the Ingalik and probably the Koyukon (Van Stone 1974). The Russian penetration of the Yukon and Kuskokwim river valleys in the 1840s set in motion major struggles over the control of trade which dramatically altered relationships among the Athabascan peoples.

Tlingit and Haidas began adapting white construction methods in the 1880s but the killer whale crest above the door indicates that this was a clan house rather than a private home.

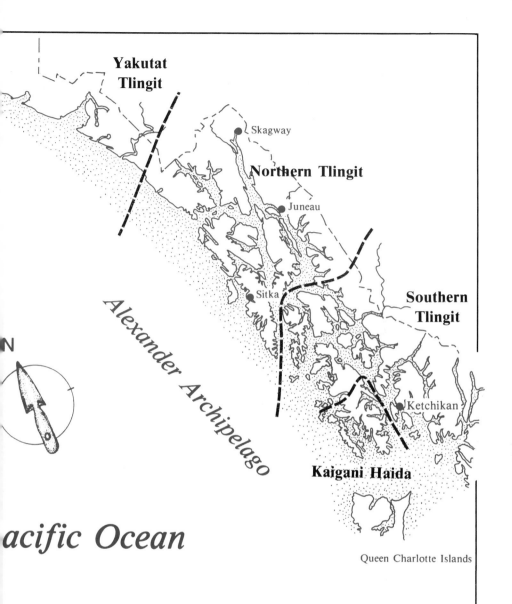

Yakutat
Tlingit

Skagway

Northern Tlingit

Juneau

Southern
Tlingit

Sitka

Alexander Archipelago

N

Ketchikan

Kaigani Haida

acific Ocean

Queen Charlotte Islands

Southeast
Coastal Indians:
Tlingit / Haida

CHAPTER 6

Southeast Coastal Indians: Tlingit and Haida

Occupying the islands and mainland of southeast Alaska are the northernmost groups of the Northwest Coast culture – the Tlingit and Haida Indians. They are well-known for their distinctive art represented in totem poles and other elegantly carved objects.

The Tlingit and Haida are more similar to Indians along the coast of present day British Columbia than to other Alaskan groups. The Tlingit occupied the vast majority of the area from Yakutat Bay to Portland Canal while the Kaigani Haida, whose Haida relatives occupied the Queen Charlotte Islands off the north coast of British Columbia, controlled the southern half of the Prince of Wales archipelago. The two groups share similar social and cultural patterns; however, their languages are unrelated and they have distinct ethnic identities.

First settlement of the southeast

While much of the broad interior of Alaska was ice-free 20,000 years ago, the mainland and islands of southeast Alaska were covered with glaciers. Human occupation of the area began around 11,000 years ago as the glaciers retreated. The first immigrants brought small microblade tools, similar to those of the earliest settlers elsewhere in Alaska, and occupied the area from 10,000 to 7,000 years ago.

Tlingit legends speak of migrations into the area from two directions. Some groups have legends of traveling down the Skeena River in north British Columbia and then migrating by boat northward into southeast Alaska. Other groups tell of travel over the coastal mountains or down the river valleys to the coast. The Kaigani Haida are much more recent immigrants to southeast Alaska having invaded the southern portion of the Prince of Wales archipelago probably less than 200 years before European contact.

It is likely that the distinctive elements of Northwest Coast culture – emphasis on woodworking, relatively permanent settlement, primary dependence on salmon, social stratification, wealth and art emerged between 2–4,000 years ago in southeast Alaska.

Population and distribution

The Tlingit were divided into 13 units, sometimes erroneously labelled "tribes" (they were not tribes because there was no political unity at this level) to which the suffix "kwan" was applied. This terminology defines a group of people who lived in a region, shared residence in several communities, intermarried, and were at peace.

The total Tlingit population was about 15,000 at the time of contact. The most numerous groups were those living on the Stikine and Chilkat rivers. The Kaigani Haida population was about 1,800 people at the time of European contact.

The Tlingit and Haida had similar settlement patterns which included relatively permanent winter villages occupied from October or November to March. From these villages, small groups of people dispersed to seasonal camps during the spring, summer and early fall.

Food and diet

The seasonal activities differed somewhat for groups who lived on the mainland from those who occupied the outer islands.

On the mainland, rivers with large runs of salmon allowed the people to remain in their villages longer. In the spring, eulachon were caught, rendered to an oil and then congealed into a grease which was a highly desired condiment eaten with dried salmon or herring eggs. Moose and mountain goat were also available on the mainland and hunted in the fall.

On the islands, streams with smaller runs of salmon required greater dispersion of the population. Marine resources were more important. In the spring, people began by taking herring and bird eggs, followed by seaweed and then halibut. Seals were hunted at rookeries at various times. In the fall, deer were hunted on the islands.

For both mainland and island groups, from late June to October, salmon were dried or smoked and stored in cedar bark or spruce root baskets for winter. Late summer and fall brought berry picking in both locales. Brown or black bear, were occasionally killed in both areas.

An important backup food supply used in winter by almost all groups were intertidal resources such as clams, cockles and chitons. Whales and sea lions apparently were not hunted by either Tlingit or Haida prior to contact although both groups occasionally used beached specimens.

Tools

Major Tlingit and Haida woodworking tools were adzes, mauls and wedges. The sharp points and cutting edges were crafted from stone, bone and shell allowing carvers to skillfully fashion red cedar into everything from spoons to houses. 61

A strong spirit was needed to overcome the strength of the halibut. Tlingit composite hooks were carved to attract power that would assist the fishermen. Lines were made of cedar bark and floats were made from seal bladders or wood.

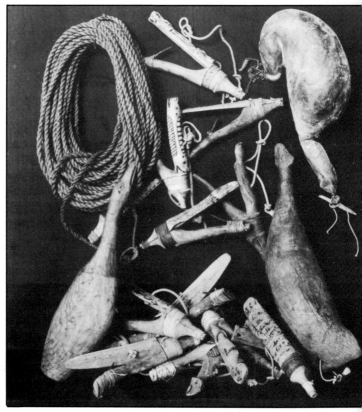

Hunting methods

Hunting was done with bows, arrows and spears for land animals while clubs were used on harbor seals which were usually taken on land.

Elaborate devices were constructed to harvest salmon. Semicircular intertidal stone traps were used to take advantage of tidal action; salmon would come in at high tide only to be caught behind the stone walls as the tide receded. A combination of ingenious wooden weirs and traps caught the salmon in the streams and rivers. Other techniques used to capture salmon included dip nets, spears and gaff hooks, the later being preferred in the swift turbid waters of mainland rivers. Men were responsible for catching and women and children for processing.

For ocean species such as halibut, cod and red snapper (a type of rockfish), the Tlingit and Haida used a composite hook consisting of two pieces of wood, yellow cedar and yew. A bone barb was lashed with cedar withes to the harder yew arm; the hook was attached to lines of processed kelp or spruce root and dropped to the bottom of the ocean. A wooden or sealskin float bobbed at the surface when a fish bit the hook. Halibut hooks were carved to show respect for the halibut and special clubs were made for dispatching this powerful fish when it was brought up.

Transportation

The Tlingit and Haida used two basic kinds of cedar dugout canoes for transportation. A small 10–16 foot model with a u-shaped bottom was designed for short, local trips and carried fewer than six people. Much larger canoes, ranging from 20 to 50 feet in length, were used for long distance travel, transport, trade and warfare. These were deep draft, v-shaped vessels. Large separate prow and stern pieces were attached to the main body with cedar withes. The prow and occasionally the sides were carved and painted with the artistic motifs of the owner. Canoes were propelled through the water by diamond-shaped paddles which both men and women could wield superbly. Sails were not used prior to contact with Europeans. The Haida of the Queen Charlotte Islands were renowned as the best canoe makers on the coast because these islands had the largest red cedar stands.

Chief Sonihat of Kasaan presented this Haida war canoe to Gov. Brady and Alaska. It presently rests on the green at Ft. Chilkoot near Haines. Photo taken about 1904.

House types

Tlingit and Haida winter dwellings were impressive structures. Their gabled, nearly square, cedar plank houses were as big as 40 feet by 60 feet but the more standard size was 20 feet by 30 feet. Typical homes consisted of four large interior

Totem Poles

The totem pole has long been used as a striking and bold symbol of Alaska Natives even though they are only found among the Tlingit and Haida. These exquisitely carved sculptures in red cedar memorialized different events in the history of a person, drawing on the crests and images owned by his clan. They were not images of deities or icons of worship as a number of early missionaries mistakenly thought.

Precise and standard principles such as split representations of animals, formlines and ovoids created a unique art considered by the famous French anthropologist Claude Levi-Strauss to rival that of Greece and Egypt. The art form was also expressed in a variety of other objects such as masks, bowls, boxes, spoons and hats.

The earliest carved poles were probably *house posts* (the main interior supporting posts around which the wooden plank houses were built) or *mortuary posts* (erected in memory of a deceased clan head often having a niche carved in the back for placement of the ashes of the deceased). These poles were usually simple, with only one or two images.

Metal tools and wealth obtained through trade with Europeans led to a proliferation of poles in the 19th century. *Free standing poles* and *portal poles* (forming the door to a house) with interlocking images and greater complexity soon became commonplace. New themes appeared too. Free-standing poles were erected to shame another person or group for actions like failure to pay debts. Even Europeans and Americans came to appear on some totem poles. Chief Skowl, a Kaigani Haida, erected a pole with carved images of Russian Orthodox priests to memorialize his opposition to Christian beliefs.

The explosion of totem pole building ceased in the late 19th century when the Tlingit and Haida came under the influence of missionaries. Many poles were destroyed or abandoned as groups left their old villages to consolidate in larger communities. In the 1930s a number of Tlingit, Haida and Tsimshian men were hired by the Civilian Conservation Corps to move and renovate some of the older poles. Totem parks were established at Saxman (outside Ketchikan), Klawock, Hydaburg and elsewhere. In the 1970s, the largest pole ever raised was erected in Kake symbolizing the resurgence of interest in traditional art by the Tlingit and Haida.

house posts, many of which were carved. Grooves on the top seated the massive beams which extended from front to back. Overlapping planks were placed on top of the rafters with a smokehole left in the center.

For most houses, the interior included a central excavated, rectangular area for a large single hearth. At ground level around the outside of the interior, low-rising platforms served as living quarters. Bark mats provided screening for privacy.

The head of the house generally occupied the quarters along the back wall opposite the entrance. Twenty to 30 people in four to six families typically occupied such houses and acted as an economic unit. The houses faced the ocean and were usually built in locations that were well protected from storms and had good beaches for landing and launching canoes.

Seasonal dwellings varied from simple lean-tos to small versions of winter homes. Among the Kaigani Haida, planks were transported from winter village dwellings to the important seasonal sites and used with house posts erected there.

Tlingit houses were used for smoking and drying fish. The lip labret worn by the woman behind the fire was considered grotesque by European standards.

Defensive sites, sometimes called forts, were common. These were typically located on steep promontories or islands where a group could go if they were under attack. Palisades, walls of logs, were sometimes erected around these sites to provide further protection. Smaller cedar or spruce houses provided shelter inside the forts.

Clothing and decoration

Everyday clothing was not particularly elaborate. In most seasons, men wore a deer or caribou skin loincloth. Conical rain hats often embellished with designs were woven out of split spruce roots by the women. Women wore skirts woven from the inner bark of the cedar tree, a remarkably soft and pliant substance when worked by skilled persons. Cloaks made of sea otter fur or cedar bark served as outer garments for men and women, but neither normally wore footgear of any kind.

Special clothing was worn for ceremony and warfare. A leader's ceremonial garb included headdress with a front-spiece carved out of wood and decorated with abalone shell, sea lion whiskers and sometimes ermine skin pelts. White pelts flowing down the leader's back gave him an extremely impressive appearance. A small bowl full of white eagle down was seated in the top of the head gear. The feathers would fly up and drift down during quick dancing motions of the wearer and was considered a sign of welcome and peaceful intent.

One of the most distinctive items of Tlingit and Haida garb was the Chilkat robe. This was a garment woven by women based on a totemic design drawn by men. It was made out of mountain goat wool and cedar bark strips. Fringed strands of wool dangled from the bottom of the blanket and dyes produced the standard yellow and black coloration. Robes were worn or displayed on ceremonial occasions and demonstrated the great wealth of the owner. Although origi-nally developed by the Tsimshian, the Chilkat Tlingit paid for the right to weave the blankets and became specialists in their production. They were highly valued along the Northwest Coast and were a major trade item.

Special garments were used by both the Tlingit and Haida for warfare. Armor constructed of slat rods woven together or thick moose or elk hide were worn as chest protectors. Wooden helmets were also worn. Principal weapons included thrusting spears, daggers, clubs, and axes.

Personal adornment for both groups included facial painting for men and labrets and nose pins for the women. Body tatooing was common among the Haida, especially for high status women.

Social organization   Social organization among the Tlingit and Haida was the most formal and structured of any Alaskan Native group. Matrilineal descent determined group membership, inheritance of leadership and wealth. Both societies were divided into two matrilineal moieties, Raven and Eagle or Wolf. An individual was a member of one or the other "side" and had to obtain a marriage partner from the opposite side; to marry or have sexual relations with a member of one's own moiety was considered incestuous.

Matrilineal *clans* were found in both groups; there were about 70–80 Tlingit clans and eight to ten Kaigani Haida clans at the time of contact. Individuals were born into these totemic corporate groups which traced their origins from mythical or legendary incidents.

The clans were typically named after an animal or mythical being. For example the Kiksadi, an important clan among the Sitka people, claimed the frog as its major symbol or crest. This symbol was used on clothing, blankets, poles, bowls, spoons and other property of members of the clan and was not be used by people belonging to other clans. Appropriation of crests and symbols were considered thefts and could result in violence between groups.

Clans were the most crucial units in Tlingit and Haida society since they held ownership to property – houses, fishing grounds, canoes, crests, ceremonial garments, dances, songs and stories. Property concepts were highly developed and respected in both Tlingit and Haida society.

In some communities, clans grew so large that all their members could not live in a single dwelling; in such cases, multiple houses of a single clan came to exist. In these cases, each house was given a special name, and the *house group* became the primary social unit in a person's life. The head of a Tlingit house was called the *hitsati* and was responsible for the well-being of all those living in the house.

Tlingit and Haida societies were stratified, meaning that there existed clearly identifiable classes of people. Classes are usually divided into the nobles or aristocracy (the *anyeti* among the Tlingit), the commoners and the slaves. Members of the aristocracy were the leaders of the clans and houses and acted as trustees over clan property for the other members. Young men and women of this class were taught special lore and behavior concerning ceremonial activities and their ancestral heritage. Typically long-standing relationships were established between two clans in opposite moieties who would intermarry over generations. This served to concentrate the wealth of both groups into a small group. For this reason, marriages, particularly among the nobles, were arranged by the mother and her brother for the woman's children.

One of the results of matrilineal descent combined with male leadership was the practice known as the *avunculate*. At marriage, a woman went to live in her husband's home. Her offspring, however, would move back to live with her brother in mid-childhood because the mother's brother (uncle) was primarily responsible for the upbringing of the children with the assistance of his mother. High status eldest nephews would likely inherit the position of their *hitsati* uncle unless they showed an inability to cope with knowledge or organizational and leadership demands of the position during training. Eventually the younger brothers and sisters became the commoner class.

Slaves were fairly numerous and were important in both trade and providing labor. They drew water, hauled wood, repaired fish traps, caught and put up fish and otherwise carried out many of the drudgeries of daily life. They were also important at potlatches when they might either be killed or released.

Ceremonies   The major ceremonial institution among the Tlingit and Haida was the potlatch. This was staged with great pomp and ceremony, primarily to honor a deceased person but also to demonstrate the clan's status and the competence of the heir. Due to a combination of grieving and fear of the corpse, Tlingit clansmen did not handle arrangements for the interment of their dead. Rather the members of the opposite moiety, typically those of the clan with which long-established ties existed, would take care of the body and details of the burial or cremation, depending on the status of the dead person's position. Most were cremated but shamans would be interred in coffins away from the community.

About a year later, the heirs of the deceased would invite those who carried out the burial work and other clan members from the opposite moiety to the potlatch. Goods, wealth and foods which had been accumulated during the intervening year were distributed in memory of the deceased individual and in thanks for the efforts of the other side. This event was usually staged by the heir and symbolized his assumption of the position of the deceased. Clan crests, dances, ceremonial bowls and spoons, garments (such as Chilkat robes) would be demonstrated showing the group's properties and rights. Perhaps the most important wealth

Hats came in both everyday and ceremonial styles. The circles and ermine skin on the top of the decorated hat indicate that it belonged to a chief who gave four potlatches in his life.

Tlingit and Haida artisans worked a variety of materials to craft a wide range of elaborate goods including baskets, bracelets, bowls, spoons, rattles, daggers, masks, paddles, hats, drums, dolls and Chilkat robes. The miniature canoes and totems were made for the tourist trade.

The Tlingit and Haida Indians were accomplished traders even before the arrival of the whites. The women adapted their basketmaking and trading skills to cater to the early tourist traffic which began in the 1880s in southeast Alaska.

items were *coppers*, pieces of copper pounded flat and engraved with totemic symbols. It is not clear if such objects existed in the precontact era, but with the introduction of sheet copper from Europeans, they began to proliferate. Usually a *mortuary pole* was commissioned and raised during the potlatch.

Potlatches expressed strong reciprocal and competitive elements. Those who gave the most attained high status through the lore which recognized their generosity. This was symbolized in special potlatch hats with rings indicating the number of potlatches an individual had sponsored. Those who were invited guests at one potlatch would be hosts later to the same people due to the division of labor between the moieties and the obligations which linked the clans together.

Potlatches were held on other occasions such as naming ceremonies, weddings, house-raising ceremonies (especially among the Haida), raising special totem poles and eradicating shameful or embarrassing incidents.

Warfare

Warfare was a common practice among both Tlingit and Haida. Motivations included obtaining wealth (including slaves) and righting perceived wrongs. Feuding, the perpetuation of multi-generation hostilities between two clan groups, was also well known. Most hostilities took the form of raids and ambushes. The Haida were considered the fiercest raiders of the coast, ranging as far south as Puget Sound in pursuit of slaves and booty, possibly due to population pressures on resources in the Queen Charlotte Islands.

Trade
Trade was highly developed among both groups and was enhanced by the ease of long-distance travel over the relatively well-protected waterways of the coast. The Tlingit obtained caribou skins, clothing and copper from interior Athabascan groups in exchange for eulachon grease, dried halibut, Chilkat robes and carved cedar objects. Haidas traded their famous canoes as well as slaves and dried halibut. A major event for both groups was the trade fair which occurred each spring at the mouth of the Nass River. Groups from all parts of the Northwest Coast traveled here to trade, put up eulachon grease, gamble and seek marriage partners.

Beliefs
The belief systems of both the Tlingit and Haida were linked to the Raven, a supernatural trickster through whose activities most of the universe's features came to be. Other animals were also important as actors in Tlingit and Haida myth and legend; particularly important were bears, the Thunderbird and a variety of other mythical beings and spirits whose acts influenced human affairs.

Both cultures had a strong belief in reincarnation which was identified by dreams and physical or behavioral similarities of new born children to some recently deceased person.

The shaman (Tlingit – *ixt*) was a powerful personage in both societies as a communicator with powerful spirits, curer and foreteller of future events. Shamans were thought to travel great distances to see events in other communities and do battle with other shamans. They were well-paid specialists who had apprentices to assist them.

Contact with Europeans
The strong organization and military experience of the Tlingit enabled them to retain their independence in the face of the Russian invasion of the their territory around 1800. The Russians were able to establish a permanent foothold at Sitka in 1805 after having initially been driven from the area by the Tlingit under the leadership of Katlian in 1802. However, they exercised little military control over the Tlingit in Sitka and none over any other Tlingit or Haida group. An important element in the retention of Tlingit independence was their ability to obtain arms and ammunition from British and American traders who wished to see the Russians driven completely from the area.

CHAPTER 7
Historic Change

Alaskan Native cultures changed slowly through the centuries in response to population increases, migration, war and trade. However, contact with Europeans brought dramatic and more far reaching changes than anything that had ever happened previously. The Russians were the first to come in pursuit of sea otters and the profits that could be obtained from trading the pelt of this beautiful and charming animal. The Aleut were first subjugated, then decimated by disease, and finally the survivors were incorporated into Russian culture through the efforts of Russian Orthodox missionaries. The Russians competed among themselves for sea otter and rapidly depleted the animals in the Aleutian Islands. This caused them to search eastward for more pelts.

In 1778, James Cook sailed as far north as Cook Inlet and his reports of the rich trade in sea otter pelts set off a mad scramble. English and American entrepreneurs sailed for the fabled Northwest Coast in pursuit of fortune. American traders armed the Tlingit and Haida, giving them the wherewithal to withstand Russian attempts to dominate the area. Although the Russians were able to establish a foothold at Sitka in 1805 after having been driven out by the Tlingit in 1802, they were never able to exercise control over the other Tlingit and Haida villages.

Sea otter slaughter ends but other trade continues

The maritime sea otter trade declined about 1815 with the extirpation of the animals virtually throughout their entire range on the west coast of North America. This resulted in a shift to trade based on terrestrial fur bearers such as beaver, mink, marten and fox. Between 1820 and 1840, the Russians gradually expanded up the coast of western Alaska establishing posts among the Bering Sea mainland Yuit in Bristol Bay, at the mouth of the Yukon River and on the Kuskokwim River. Russian methods had changed by this time with severe terms of trade and missionaries replacing outright subjugation. But in the middle Yukon and Norton Sound areas, the Russians encountered an already flourishing trading system which diverted furs from interior Alaskan Athabascan groups to the Siberian Chukchi through coastal Inupiat middlemen. In addition, English overland traders expanded westward out of Canada and established a trading post at Fort Yukon in 1847. These competitors severely constricted Russian expansion and with the decline in the profitability of trade in the coastal region, the entire American venture became a financial burden on the Russian crown.

The legacy of the Russian period included smallpox and venereal disease that wreaked great havoc throughout the southern coastal regions. The Aleut and Koniag populations were reduced to approximately 20 percent of the precontact level while the Chugach, Tlingit, Haida and Tanaina may have been reduced by 50 percent. This caused a consolidation of the population. Intermarriage resulted in many Alaska Natives with Russian names. Literacy in their own languages was created among the Aleut, Koniag and a few Tlingit through the efforts of Russian Orthodox missionaries to translate the Bible.

Russia sells Alaska to U.S. but little changes

Russian imperial disenchantment with the American colony resulted in the sale of Alaska to the United States in 1867 for $7.2 million dollars. The Tongass Tlingit group objected strenuously to the sale rightly noting that the Russians could not sell what they did not own. But these protestations had no effect on a government and people bent on a mission of manifest destiny and the civilization of the American Indian.

From 1867 to 1884, Alaska had no civil government coming under the military jurisdiction of first the Army and then the Navy. The outposts were manned by an extremely uncouth and rugged breed of soldier who apparently contributed substantially to the difficulties of the Native groups. One of the results of the military presence was teaching the Tlingit how to make homebrew or "hootchinoo." But more importantly at Kake and Angoon, Tlingits seeking to rectify injustices were given a lesson in the military might and will of the U.S. government. These villages were shelled with houses, canoes and other facilities destroyed. The independent Tlingit and Haida, brought up short by this devastation, realized that their days of independence were numbered and some form of accommodation was going to be necessary to survive.

A few whites from the United States began filtering into Alaska after the purchase, some as prospectors, some as whalers, some as store keepers and some as fish processors salting salmon for sale on the west coast. These adventurers and entrepreneurs established new avenues of accommodation—trade and labor.

In the far north, the Inupiat were exposed to Yankee whalers from the 1850s through the 1880s. This contact brought new material goods, opportunities for trade and labor, and diseases which decimated the north coast in the 1880s. The destruction of the bowhead whale and walrus by Yankee whalers combined with bad weather led to the starvation of 1500 St. Lawrence Island Eskimos in the winter of 1878–79, reducing the population by 75 percent.

Salmon canneries prove to be a mixed blessing

In 1878, the new technique of canning salmon came to Alaska and within ten years canneries were built on many of the Natives' most important fishing grounds. In some places the canneries brought opportunities for men to work as fishermen and women to work in the processing. But in other places, notably Bristol Bay, Natives were excluded from the labor force since imported Chinese were regarded as more tractable and reliable. Unfortunately, the cannery owners gave little consideration to the needs of the Natives and many salmon runs were devastated by the turn of the century despite Native complaints to U.S. fisheries agents. Although laws were passed to protect the fish, those same laws outlawed traditional Native fishing practices and subjected them to arrest by federal agents. Despite these problems, commercial fishing as a way of life became deeply embedded in many southern coastal Tlingit, Haida, Koniag and Bristol Bay Yuit communities by 1900.

Missionaries arrive; English replaces Russian language in schools

Another avenue of accommodation was provided by the missionary educators. Sheldon Jackson was a Presbyterian missionary who visited Alaska in 1877 and returned to the United States with a vision of establishing missionary educators in villages to carry out the Christianization and education of the Natives.

One of the key elements in the American missionary plan was the eradication of Native languages and their replacement by English. Students were prohibited from speaking their Native tongues in school and were often harshly punished if the rule was broken. After the turn of the century Jackson was removed as Special Agent for Education due to growing disapproval of the use of federal funds to promote religious schools and organizations. Nevertheless, his ideas and efforts established a powerful template in the minds of non-Natives and many Natives for how cultural change and development should proceed for Alaska Natives.

The gold rush to the Klondike, Nome and other Alaskan locales brought a huge influx of whites to the territory. The Organic Act of 1884 recognized Natives rights to their homes and camps and stipulated that they were not to be disturbed in their use of those sites. However, in 1891 Congress allowed whites to begin applying for title to business sites and many Native properties were taken as a result, particularly by canneries. Natives were not citizens and therefore had no recourse to obtain title to lands. The influx of whites and the inability of Natives to stake claims to mines further clarified their vulnerable, second-class status under U.S. laws. This led to a strong desire to obtain citizenship so that property rights could be obtained and protected.

New Archangel (Sitka) about 1840. Litho by Friedrich Heinrich von Kittlitz.

The struggle for land claims was born out of the southeast Alaskan experience. President Theodore Roosevelt had placed the vast majority of the timbered lands of southeast and southcentral Alaska into the Tongass and Chugach National Forests. White settlers had established canneries and communities on Native lands. This injustice led to resentment and conviction to regain what was lost among many Natives. Congressional legislation was passed in 1935 authorizing the Tlingit and Haida to pursue land claims.

Similar concerns were also voiced by the interior Athabascan people in 1915 where they met with Alaskan Congressional delegate James Wickersham at the first Tanana Chiefs Conference. The chiefs complained about the

Throughout southern Alaska, Native women provided labor on the gurry lines of many salmon canneries which operated during the latter part of the 19th century. Their husbands ran the fishing boats which caught the fish the women canned.

hunting lands and fishing stations being disrupted by white prospectors. Other whites were trapping on customary Indian trap lines causing further economic hardship. Wickersham told the chiefs that they could have homesteads or reservations, but that in order to survive they must become civilized like the white man. The chiefs told him that neither homesteads nor reservations made sense to them; all they wanted was to be left alone. But that was not to be.

Some areas remain isolated but disease strikes everywhere

In northern and western Alaska, beyond the reach of the commercial salmon industry, the pace of cultural change was much slower due to the lack of resources attracting the economic interests of whites. After the collapse of commercial whaling in the 1890s, coastal northwest Alaska experienced little contact with outsiders. Yuit peoples of the Yukon-Kuskokwim delta and St. Lawrence Island areas never had any true boom and their isolation has allowed them to retain their language and more of their cultural traditions than other Alaskan Native people.

But no Alaska Native groups were able to escape the ravages of disease. Major causes were influenza and tuberculosis. The Native population declined to its lowest point in

1909 when the census recorded 25,331 persons. Poor housing and sanitation plus inadequate medical services resulted in continuing high death rates among Alaskan Natives until the 1950s when an extensive campaign by the U.S. Public Health Service eradicated tuberculosis and a village aid program was created to provide better primary care in the villages. The improved health care also resulted in a "baby boom" during the late 1950s and 1960s resulting in rapid population increase.

Statehood and oil bring land issues to a head

World War II brought the next major wave of white immigration to Alaska. The white population increased from 40,066 in 1939 to 94,780 in 1950. Economic decline after World War II set in motion the struggle for statehood, driven fundamentally by Alaskan whites desires to control the resources of the territory.

The Alaska Statehood Act was passed in 1958 and provided for the new state to select 108 million of Alaska's 375 million acres. These selections, which often were made over customary and traditional Native lands, galvanized Natives throughout Alaska to organize into regional associations and protest the taking of their lands.

The dilemmas which the new state posed for Alaska Natives led to the formation of the Alaska Federation of Natives (AFN) in 1966 to pursue the struggle for land claims with the federal government. This organization began lobbying Congress and succeeded in convincing Secretary of the Interior Udall to suspend state land selections in 1966 until Native claims had been settled. In 1968, the giant oil discovery on the North Slope brought the crisis to a head. With Native claims clouding the title to the land, oil development could not proceed. Native, State and oil corporation leaders all wanted the land claims issue solved. The final outcome was the Alaska Native Claims Settlement Act (ANCSA) signed into law by President Nixon on December 18, 1971.

ANCSA becomes unique experiment

ANCSA provided a cash settlement of $962.5 million and 44 million acres distributed to 12 regional and about 200 village corporations. Individual Alaskan Natives alive on December 18, 1971 were enrolled in the corporations based on where they were born or lived and were given 100 shares of stock. Most Alaskan Natives are members of both a village and regional corporation.

ANCSA also explicitly extinguished all aboriginal hunting and fishing rights, revoked all previous reservations

(except the Tsimshian reservation on Metlakatla) and re
iterated the continuing "trust" responsibility of the federal
government to protect Alaska Natives. Despite extinguishing
fishing and hunting rights, Congress declared that it expected
the Department of the Interior and the State of Alaska to
provide for the "subsistence needs" of Alaska Natives. This
has become a major controversy in Alaska between Natives
and non-Natives, rural and urban residents.

ANCSA is a unique experiment in settling land claims
and establishing institutions for Native American groups. It
was intended by Congress to provide a vehicle for economic
development and assimilation. But it has not been an eco
nomic success and few Natives wish to be totally assimilated.
Few of the regional corporations have been successful while
at least two are faced with bankruptcy and loss of lands.
Village corporations have even less chance of surviving.
Major concerns at the present are loss of lands due to
bankruptcy or taxation, loss of Native control after 1991 when
shares in the corporations can be sold, and the exclusion of
those born since 1971 from the corporations (Berger 1985).
Alaska Natives have proposed amendments to ANCSA to
address these problems.

While some Native Alaskans are assuming jobs in the cities, many still practice a traditional subsistence lifestyle in Alaska's rural villages. *(Photo by Kathy Kiefer.)*

These concerns have also led to a new movement for tribal recognition and control of lands. The "tribal sovereignty" movement is especially strong among the Yuit of the Yukon-Kuskokwim delta where the concept of a Yupiit Nation has emerged.

Natives now face uncertain future

The decade and a half since 1971 has seen dramatic changes in Alaska Native life. Better health care has allowed Native populations to recover to 64,357 as of 1980. Improved housing, village schools and gymnasiums, television and many amenities of modern urban life have been imported to village Alaska. Some Natives have moved to the cities. But these changes have largely been the result of Alaska's oil wealth and federal programs and not of development due to ANCSA.

Rapid culture change has assaulted adaptations worked out over 200 generations and has produced "future shock" in many Alaskan Native populations. Problems include alcoholism, diabetes and heart disease due to altered diets, increases in child and wife abuse, and the highest suicide rates in the nation. Despite improvements in earnings, Alaska Natives still dominate the poverty statistics and have the highest rates of unemployment in Alaska. Native youth are faced with excruciating decisions about how to integrate the activities, traditions and values of the elders with the demands of the modern world.

Alaska Natives are poised at a crucial juncture in their history. Economic and social conditions are difficult and in some places nearly desperate. Political relationships with the state and federal government are anxious and ambiguous. Only time will tell if Native peoples will persist through their adaptability and thrive in their ancestral lands, gradually disappear as culturally distinct peoples into larger American society, or be shunted into the stigmatized ranks of the unemployed and poverty-stricken. Although Alaska Native peoples have some influence in determining that future, a much larger role will be played by other Americans who will establish the crucial rules under which Alaska Natives will live through the Congress and the courts of the United States. We all are share responsibility for the future of Alaska Native peoples.

References

Chapter 1: Introduction
Damas, David (ed.). 1984. *Handbook of North American Indians, Vol. 5: Arctic.* Washington, D.C.: Smithsonian Institution.
Dumond, Donald. 1977. *The Eskimos and Aleuts.* London: Thames and Hudson.
Helm, June (ed.). 1981. *Handbook of North American Indians, Vol. 6: Subarctic.* Washington, D.C.: Smithsonian Institution.

Chapter 2: Aleuts
Black, Lydia. 1980. Early History. *In* The Aleutians, L. Morgan (ed.). *Alaska Geographic* 7(3):82-105.
Lantis, Margaret. 1984. Aleut. *In* Damas, D. (ed.). *Handbook of North American Indians, Vol. 5: Arctic.* pp. 161-184.
Laughlin, William. 1980. *Aleuts: Survivors of the Bering Land Bridge.* New York: Holt, Rinehart and Winston.

Chapter 3: Northern Eskimos: Inupiat
Burch, Ernest. 1984. Kotzebue Sound Eskimo. *In* Damas, D. (ed.). *Handbook of North American Indians, Vol. 5: Arctic.* pp. 303-319.
Hall, Edward. 1984. Interior North Alaska Eskimo. *In* Damas, D. (ed.). *Handbook of North American Indians, Vol. 5: Arctic.* pp. 338-346.
Oswalt, Wendell. 1967. *Alaskan Eskimos.* Scranton, Penn.: Chandler Publishing Company.

Chapter 4: Southern Eskimos: Yuit
Clark, Donald. 1984. Pacific Eskimo: Historical Ethnography. *In* Damas, D. (ed.). *Handbook of North American Indians, Vol. 5: Arctic.* pp. 185-197.
Feinup-Riordan, Ann. 1983. *The Nelson Island Eskimo.* Anchorage: Alaska Pacific University Press.
Hughes, Charles. 1984. Saint Lawrence Island Eskimo. *In* Damas, D. (ed.). *Handbook of North American Indians, Vol. 5: Arctic.* pp. 262-277.
Van Stone, James. 1984. Mainland Southwest Alaska Eskimo. *In* Damas, D. (ed.). *Handbook of North American Indians, Vol. 5: Arctic.* pp. 224-242.

Chapter 5: Interior Indians: Athabascans
Simeone, William. 1982. *A History of Alaskan Athapaskans.* Anchorage: Alaska Historical Commission.
Slobodin, James. 1981. Kutchin. *In* Helm, J. (ed.). *Handbook of North American Indians, Vol. 6: Subarctic.* pp. 514-532.
Van Stone, James. 1974. *Athapaskan Adaptations.* Chicago: Aldine Publishing Company.

Chapter 6: Southeast Coastal Indians: Tlingit and Haida
Drucker, Philip. 1955. *Indians of the Northwest Coast.* New York: American Museum of Natural History.
Oberg, Kalervo. 1973. *The Social Economy of the Tlingit Indians.* Seattle: University of Washington Press.

Chapter 7: Historic Change
Arnold, Robert et al. 1976. *Alaska Native Land Claims.* Anchorage: Alaska Native Foundation.
Berger, Thomas. 1985. *Village Journey.* New York: Hill and Wang.
Case, David. 1984. *Alaska Natives and American Laws.* Fairbanks: University of Alaska Press.
Hinckley, Ted. 1972. *The Americanization of Alaska, 1867-1897.* Palo Alto, Ca.: Pacific Books.